The Technique

The Technique of Weaving

John Tovey

B. T. Batsford Limited
London

© John Tovey 1965 and 1975
First published 1965
New edition 1975
First published in paperback 1983
Reprinted 1989

ISBN 0 7134 3851 7 (paperback)

Printed in Great Britain by
Courier International Ltd, Tiptree, Essex
for the publishers
B T Batsford Limited
4 Fitzhardinge Street
London W1H 0AH

Contents

Acknowledgment

I would like to thank all those who have helped me in the preparation of this book, and in particular A. Cox for his photographic work, Catherine Cullen for the photographs for the colour plates and James Proctor for his help in preparing the looms and the models for the illustrations. My thanks are also due to the Principal of the Regional College of Art, Kingston-upon-Hull and Phyl Shillinglaw for permission to use photographs of students' work, and to John Maxwell for photographs of looms. I am especially grateful to Tadek Beutlich, Peter Collingwood, Theo Moorman, Moik Scheile, Kay Sekimachi and Vyvian Western for permission to include photographs of their work, and to my wife for her invaluable help in typing the manuscript and cross-checking technical details throughout the book.

JT

In sections I and II of this book reference is made frequently to the different parts of looms and various types. These diagrams show the three main types and the names of the important parts.

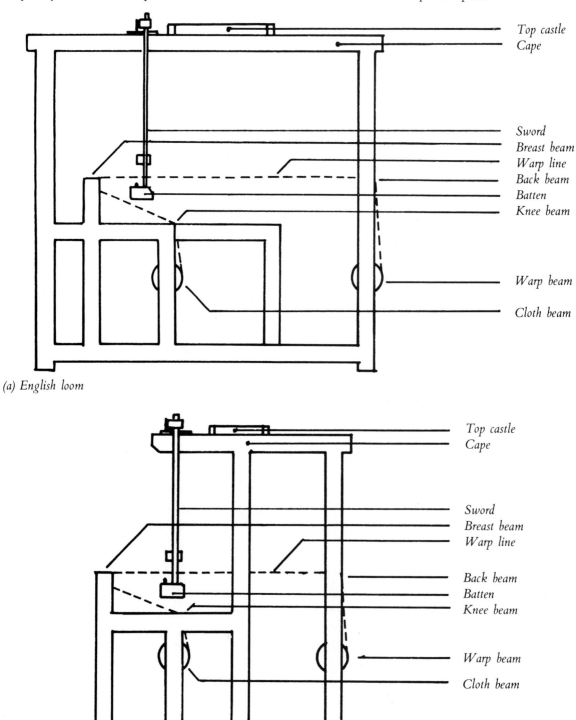

Top castle
Cape

Sword
Breast beam
Warp line
Back beam
Batten
Knee beam

Warp beam

Cloth beam

(a) English loom

Top castle
Cape

Sword
Breast beam
Warp line

Back beam
Batten
Knee beam

Warp beam

Cloth beam

(b) Swedish loom

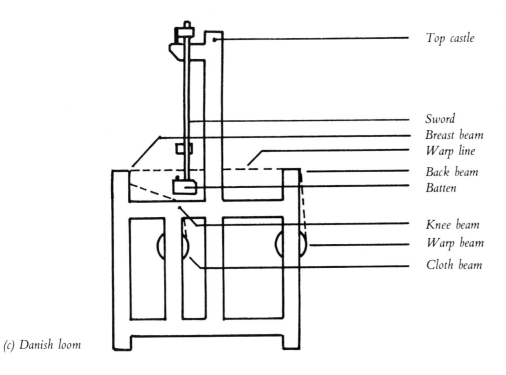

Top castle

Sword
Breast beam
Warp line
Back beam
Batten

Knee beam
Warp beam
Cloth beam

(c) Danish loom

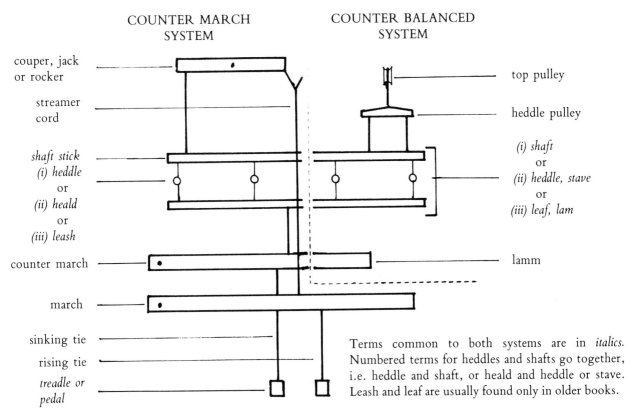

COUNTER MARCH
SYSTEM

COUNTER BALANCED
SYSTEM

couper, jack
or rocker

streamer
cord

shaft stick
(i) heddle
or
(ii) heald
or
(iii) leash

counter march

march

sinking tie

rising tie

treadle or
pedal

top pulley

heddle pulley

(i) shaft
or
(ii) heddle, stave
or
(iii) leaf, lam

lamm

Terms common to both systems are in *italics.*
Numbered terms for heddles and shafts go together,
i.e. heddle and shaft, or heald and heddle or stave.
Leash and leaf are usually found only in older books.

9

Introduction

Weaving is one of the fundamental crafts of mankind. Amongst the earliest known pieces of crude pottery are some with the imprint of the woven rush baskets into which the wet clay had been pressed, and although no such very early weaving has survived, there is no doubt as to its existence. Advances in weaving could not be made while man was still a nomad, but as soon as people had a more permanent dwelling a simple upright loom appeared. The warp hung from a horizontal branch and was weighted with clay or stone weights. Longer warps were used when the warps were placed horizontally, and finally the looms as we know them today began to appear. Weaving also took many different forms in different parts of the world, the indigenous raw materials, and materials of which the loom was made and the climate all influencing the type of fabric produced. In fact the historical and ethnological aspects of the craft provide very wide and interesting studies in themselves.

In some parts of the world hand weaving is still a living craft, and with comparatively simple tools very fine cloths are produced, cloths which are far superior to any machine woven cloth, such as the silk or cotton cloths with real gold thread that are still woven in India for saris. There is also the Scandinavian hand weaving, where production by hand of such things as rugs, curtains and cushions is still a commercial proposition.

Different parts of the world have become famous for distinctive types of fabric from very early days of the craft. Five thousand years ago the Egyptians could already weave fine cotton and linen cloths, and tapestry panels have been found in tombs three and a half thousand years old. India and China were early famous for their silks, and the Asiatic royalty contemporary with Alexander the Great wore silk heavily ornamented with gold thread.

Palermo in Sicily was famous for its silks and cloth of gold from the mid-ninth century until Sicily fell to the French in 1266, when several of the Italian states took its place in turn. Florence produced some of the finest velvets and brocades of silk and gold ever known, until she fell in 1530. This period is often regarded as the summit of human skill and artistry in textile design. France, with the establishment of the silk industry at Lyons in the early sixteenth century soon became, and still is the chief centre for silk weaving in Europe.

England during this period had built up a wide reputation for the excellence of its wool. Even before the Roman Conquest very fine woollen cloth was being woven at Winchester, and by A.D. 300 was being exported as far as Eastern Europe, but after the Romans left the wool trade declined badly. With the coming of Christianity the wool trade revived; as the monasteries were established the monks were able to rear their flocks in a settled community. The Cistercians, by their work in bringing large areas of hitherto wild country into use as grazing land, laid down the foundations of the Yorkshire woollen industry.

The raw wool was still largely exported, and though some English cloth also went abroad, the Flemish weavers, using English fleece, were the chief woollen manufacturers. Several attempts were made to help the English woollen trade by prohibiting the import of cloth and the export of fleece, but without great success. Finally Flemish weavers were induced to settle in England and improve the quality of the cloth, which they did so successfully that by the close of the Middle Ages England had become a great cloth exporting country. This was the great period of the craft guilds, and in the wool areas of East Anglia and the Cotswolds particularly fine churches and houses built about this time are evidence of the wealth of the wool trade. Worstead, in Norfolk, was the centre of the manufacture of fine hard woollen cloth which now bears its name.

The English silk weaving industry, established in the mid fourteenth century was enlarged later by successive influxes of religious refugees from the continent, until in the eighteenth century Spitalfields was the chief European centre for silk damasks and brocades.

By the end of the seventeenth century cotton had become a great rival of wool, and a large cotton industry was in being. In 1733 John Kay's invention of the flying shuttle started the train of inventions and mechanical improvement for the wool and cotton industries. The consequent demand for more machinery and new sources of power was the beginning of the Industrial Revolution, and Britain's lead in engineering.

The craft of weaving with its many allied crafts from wool sorting to finishing, and the craft of the shepherd, have been responsible for shaping much of present day England and English history. The traditions of the craft died out almost everywhere during the Industrial Revolution, but sufficient remained in rural areas, and in the records and writings of master weavers for a very complete picture to be drawn. There is no need for us to go back to the days when harnesses of ninety shafts were often used, and fullers earth was used to absorb the grease in fulling woollens, but the tradition of the weaver as a fine craftsman, and an inventive one, is still alive, and should be maintained.

This book is an endeavour to present the traditional techniques of weavers such as John Murphy and later Luther Hooper as applied to present day hand weaving. There are many books dealing with design, and with the beginnings of the craft and giving pattern drafts and instructions for weaving various articles. This is an attempt to fill the gap between the general books and the technical books written primarily for industrial use, and should be of use to any hand weaver wishing to go more deeply into the craft, as well as students.

The weaver must have full understanding of the equipment and materials to use them to the best advantage. Good weaving depends on meticulous attention to detail, and sufficient skill to perform all the various processes without conscious effort, but not without thought. Weaving should be a pleasure, not a battle of wits with a tangled warp or a reluctant loom. The weaver should be able to express his ideas freely, without having to put all his thought into the mechanics of production, and there is tremendous scope for the artist once the craftsmen's skill has

been acquired, but that is beyond the scope of this book.

The book is divided into four parts. The first deals with the apparatus of weaving, looms and ancillary equipment, with a description of each, the names of its various parts, and the merits or disadvantages of different types performing a similar function. Any terms used in later sections will be explained there. Part two covers the preliminary processes and the actual weaving. Each sub-section begins with a description of the process, and then describes in detail how it is carried out on each type of equipment. The theory is dealt with in part three: calculations, weaves and 'loose warp' techniques. The final part covers the specialised techniques for the rigid heddle and table looms.

Many weavers will have learnt to carry out these processes in other ways; it is not suggested that this book gives the only way, but a way that is quick and efficient for each process, and the more efficiently and accurately the preliminary work is done, the more time is available for creative work, and the more satisfaction will be derived from it. We are able to call on the inherited skills and traditions passed on for hundreds of years, and this heritage should not be ignored. Often the preliminary processes are done slowly and inefficiently merely because the trouble cannot be taken to learn to do them well, in the mistaken idea that it is easier to do so, and gadgets are made to save the effort of acquiring a skill or a sense of judgement. The old weavers were very inventive, and were always ready to modify their looms and mountings to improve them for a specific purpose, and with mountings of cord and wood this is always possible, though with chains and metal it is not. This type of modification is still being made by a few skilled weavers, but is vastly different from the gadgets designed to avoid the effort necessary to acquire the elementary skills.

Types of looms

Weaving is the process of making cloth by interlacing two sets of threads running at right angles to
each other, the longitudinal threads being the warp,
and the threads across being the weft, individually
called 'ends' and 'picks'. The order of interlacing is
called the weave, and varies from very simple
'under 1 over 1' of plain weave, to the very complex
weaves of double, gauze and figured fabrics. The
loom is the frame used to hold the warp while the
weft is inserted, as well as the resulting cloth. The
simplest looms are little more than a frame and two
rollers for the warp and cloth, but the large ones are
highly complex pieces of equipment.

There are two main types of loom, the table loom,
which includes the rigid heddle, and the foot power
in its many and complex variations from the simple
four shaft to the draw loom.

1 Table looms

a The easiest of all to work is the *rigid heddle*, in
which the single piece of apparatus, the rigid heddle
itself, does the work of shedding, spacing and beating
up. The most useful type has the rollers at the
bottom of the loom and back and front rods at the
top for the warp and cloth to run over. This gives
more length to the warp and saves some of the strain
of shedding. The cheaper types without front and
back rods, as well as having a shorter length for the
warp, suffer from having no firm edge for the threads
to run over. Consequently any unevenness in the
winding on causes variation in the level of shed across
the loom.

The big drawbacks of the rigid heddles are that
they are limited to one sett, and only one weave except for grouped and spaced warps, and special techniques described in Section IV.

1a *Rigid heddle loom with metal and wooden heddles*

b The *two shaft roller heddle loom* is even more
limited, as it has the same fixed sett, but the special
weaves are impossible on it. The warp can still be
spaced or grouped, or can be given a half sett. It is
quicker weaving, and is useful for tapestry, inlay,
free shuttle and other hand techniques, as the shed
stays open without being held, and a touch on the
lever at either side changes the shed.

A two shaft loom with conventional mounting has
no advantage over the roller heddle except that the
sett can be varied. If anything it is slightly slower to
weave with.

1b *Two-shaft roller-heddle loom*

c The *four shaft mounting* in its standard form permits a wide variety of weaves and setts, and many weavers do not feel the need to go beyond it as most of the traditional weaves are four shaft, though many of the linen weaves require six or more. The well known all-over textured weaves such as honeycomb, canvas, huckaback and mock-leno are four shaft weaves or have a four shaft version. Simplified crêpe weaves, piqués, bedford cords, whipcords, simple distorted wefts and corduroys are all possible. Double plain cloth, double width plain cloth, tubular plain cloth, double weft faced twill and twill backed hopsack can be woven, though the two cloths in the double plain weave cannot be correctly stitched together. A slight modification makes gauze and leno weaving possible, and an additional back roller gives the extra warp weaves and simple warp pile weaving (velvet).

IC *Table loom with eight shafts*

d The practical limit of a shaft harness table loom is the *eight shaft mounting*. Beyond this a draw harness of twenty-five or so shafts can be used, but the draw loom has its own specialised technique. (See *Designer's Draw Loom* by Alice Hindson.)

The eight shaft loom opens up a much wider range of fancy twills and satins, more complex versions of standard weaves, and also two block (checked) cloths in double plain weave, double faced twill and a number of linen weaves using five to eight shafts.

2 Foot power looms

There are certain considerations which affect all foot power looms of whatever type of construction. Generally speaking, a large loom is easier to gate and to operate than a small one of similar design and quality. It is easy to get inside a big loom when tying up or adjusting the treadles, the mounting will be generously built with plenty of clearance between the various parts, and the warp line will be long, so saving strain on the threads when shedding. The width will be several cm (in.) greater than the reed width so that winding on will be straightforward, the warp can easily be set wider on the warp roller than the actual reed width of the cloth even when working to the full capacity, and the heddles will not always be slipping off the ends of the heddle sticks.

As a large loom is heavily built, it can have various additional fittings such as a dobby, a fly shuttle, a second back roller, giving a greater capacity for more interesting weaves and experimental weaving.

The pivoting of the batten is important. It can be slung either over or under the warp, the former being decidedly the better position. The overslung is stable, and is therefore sensitive to use, whilst the underslung being unstable falls forward onto the fell of the cloth and has to be held back for light cloths, an awkward and tiring movement to make. As the overslung swings forward the reed faces up towards the weaver, and the fell is visible; the underslung batten faces downwards as the beat is made and the cap of the batten hides the fell, making difficult the weaving of any cloth which needs to be seen whilst being woven, e.g. grouped or spaced weft. Being more loosely pivoted there is some give in the overslung batten, which is better than the rigidity of the underslung, and the overslung is easier to remove whilst threading. The vertical adjustment of the overslung is easier and finer than that of the underslung, and has also the horizontal adjustment forwards and backwards so that the length of the beat can be maintained during the weave-up. The overslung batten can be much heavier than the underslung and is therefore easier to use, the weight doing much of the work of beating up.

A more debatable point is the pivoting of the treadles, which may be at the front or back of the loom; and both positions have certain advantages. The front slung treadles are fairly firmly held in line at the point at which they are operated, so that they are easily worked over and are identifiable by position without having to look at them. The back slung are operated at their free ends, and while the foot may easily be slid from one to the other by swinging the treadles sideways till they touch, it is not so easy to jump to a treadle over intervening ones.

The front slung treadle moves in a greater arc at the back of the loom than at the front, which helps to give the greater lift or fall of the back shafts. The back slung treadles move more at the front, and therefore increase the disparity between the length of the ties.

The back slung treadle has the force applied at the end, and the weight to be moved is near the centre, therefore the foot travels twice as far as the shaft lifts, but needs only half the force. On a short loom with front slung treadles, the opposite occurs, and the treadles nearer the pivot of the marches, which are again at a mechanical disadvantage, can be quite heavy to work. A deep loom can have front slung treadles bracketed out beyond the seat of the loom, so that the force is applied nearly as far from the fulcrum as is the weight. The actual effort needed then is the same as that required to raise the shaft, and foot and shaft move by an equal amount.

Taking everything into consideration, the front slung treadles are better if the loom is deep and the treadles can be pivoted outside the loom, and back slung are better if the treadles must be kept within the loom frame and the loom is short from front to back or narrow from side to side. A very short loom, such as a foot power conversion from a table loom may need front slung treadles because of the physical impossiblity of obtaining a deep enough movement and getting the weaver's legs under the top of the loom over back slung treadles.

a   The English or four post loom   This is not in fact peculiar to England; but is merely called so for convenience. The four post loom is found everywhere, and has been in common use since the fifteenth century, both for the shaft harness and draw harness. It is the best type of loom, having all the advantages that size and heaviness of construction can give it. The only major drawback for present day weavers is the space that it requires. Often the seat is built in between the two front uprights, and is fully adjustable for height and reach, an important point often overlooked.

b   The Swedish loom   There are two versions of the Swedish loom. The original attempt to save space retained the back upright of the English type, and set the batten on a short side member supported by a

2   *English or four post loom*

3   *Swedish loom*

bracket. It lacks rigidity in the topcastle, and cannot take a heavy batten. It also is awkward to tie up as it is very difficult, if not impossible, to get inside it. Usually it is supplied with a counter balanced harness, as a counter march needs more space within the frame.

A later development was the addition of a second upright which made the side rail or cape much firmer. The batten was still cantilevered out from the upright, but was more rigid than the earlier type. This made it deeper from front to back than the earlier loom, giving a longer warp line and room to get inside the loom for adjustment as well as space for a counter march harness.

c The Danish loom The characteristic feature of the Danish loom is the single upright in the middle of the side. The harness, almost invariably counter-balanced, hangs from a tie-beam between the tops of the uprights. The batten is often underslung, with the attendant disadvantages, though it can be overslung on short cantilevered brackets. Often the back beam is omitted, the warp roller being on the warp line, which makes fine adjusting of the shedding difficult, partly because of the continually altering effective diameter of the roller as the warp sticks come round to the top, and partly because of the variation in diameter which often occurs in the winding-on. Its advantages are compactness and simplicity.

d Dobby and witch These are both devices for selecting and lifting mechanically any number of shafts to the full capacity of the machine, usually sixteen, twenty-four or thirty-two. Only one treadle is needed, the down stroke lifting the shafts already selected, and the return stroke selecting the shafts for the next pick. On both the selection is made by wooden pegs set into 'lags', wooden bars which are fastened together with metal links to form a continuous chain, which runs round a rotating barrel with grooves along its length. As the barrel rotates the lags are presented in succession to a series of long vertical hooks, one to each shaft. The shaft is fastened to a loop at the bottom, and the hook at the top is caught on a metal bar, the 'lifting knife', when a particular shaft has to be raised.

The difference between the dobby and the witch lies in the selection mechanism. The dobby has large square pegs set in large holes, and the pegs push the

4　*Danish loom*

5a　*Pattern dobby loom without dobby mechanism*

15

hooks off the lifting knife, the witch has fine straight pegs like match sticks and the hooks are pushed onto the lifting knife. The photographs show this difference; the dobby has all the hooks raised except the ones to be left down, the witch has all the hooks left down except the one to be raised. The reversing

5b *Dobby*

6 *Witch*

mechanism on a dobby has to be held whilst turning the barrel backwards for a missed pick, and as soon as it is released the spring takes it forward again. On the witch the gear can be set to run either forwards or backwards continuously, making designing and pattern weaving easier, as a short chain can be pegged, and run in either direction. A dobby is better for production, as the whole chain would be pegged and run through in the same direction.

e   The draw loom   The draw loom is a completely different type of loom, for figured work. Its use is outside the scope of this book, and the construction and operation of draw looms of several kinds is well covered by other writers.

The modern draw loom has a shaft harness of up to thirty-six shafts individually controlled by a draw monture. The two cords from the ends of each shaft run together over a pulley and down to a bar in front of the shafts. Diagram 7 shows only the first and

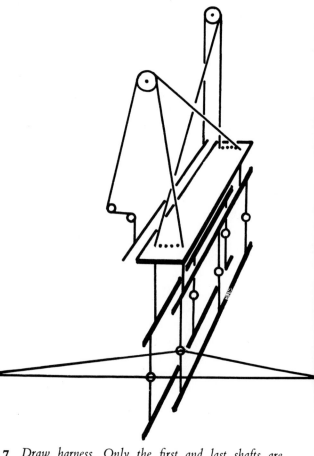

7 *Draw harness. Only the first and last shafts are shown, the latter being raised*

last of a set of shafts. When the cords are pulled out and down to the dotted position by a 'fork' (not shown), the shaft rises. Any number of shafts in any combination may be picked up on the fork and lifted, the different combinations required for each pick being kept by strings threaded through the vertical cords. A ground harness of four to eight shafts is often added in front of the pattern harness for damask weaving, etc.

The earlier draw looms worked in a similar way, but single threads instead of shafts were controlled by the vertical cords. They needed an assistant at the side of the loom to lift and hold the pattern sheds while the weaver worked over the ground treadles.

f Rug looms and frames A simple frame 15 cm (6 in.) wider and 45 cm (18 in.) longer than the size of the work is all that is needed for a rug, particularly a tufted rug in which much of the time is taken by the knotting. Shedding for the ground weave is by shed stick and leashes, and no provision is made for warps longer than the frame. Rug looms have an almost vertical warp, the warp roller being at the top, and the cloth roller about 2 ft (60 cm) from the ground, to bring the work to a convenient height. The two shafts, treadle operated, are mounted in grooves to run horizontally, and the beater is spring loaded and often held in the up position by a catch. There is very little difference in design between various rug looms.

Mountings and harnesses

The individual threads of a warp are controlled by heddles of string or wire, having an eye at the centre for the thread and loops or eyes at the ends for the shaft sticks or slider frames. The sticks are passed through the loops (doups), and a length of twine is tied from end to end of each stick to prevent the heddles from slipping off. A complete set of shafts of any number is called a harness, and the cords, levers, rollers or pulleys controlling the shafts are collectively called the mounting. Mountings are of two main types, rising shed only, and rising and sinking shed, the latter group being divisible into counter balanced and counter march actions.

1 Table looms

The simplest looms are those for plain weave only; the rigid heddle in which the heddle itself does everything, and the two shaft roller heddle (*8*) in which the individual heddles are knitted continuously to a cord along the top and bottom, and are accurately spaced to a given sett. The cords are fixed along the rollers, and the heddles laid alternate sides. The heddles can run straight or be crossed between the rollers, and turning the rollers forwards and backwards changes the shed.

a *Four shaft table looms* can have a direct lift in the centre or a lift at each side, the latter system being more efficient but entailing more work when adjusting. The connections between the shafts and the operating levers are usually of loom cord, though looms are made with chains instead. These make impossible the fine adjustment that a good weaver prefers to make for himself, and completely lack resilience, but do save trouble for coarse work.

a (i) The lift at the centre can be applied either directly through a single cord on smaller looms, or through a bow cord which balances the shafts better on a larger loom. The cord can be raised by a knob which is pulled sideways over a slotted block which receives the cords, the knob preventing the cord from sliding back, but an easier method to work employs two sets of pulleys so that the knob can be pulled downwards outside the loom frame, or can be replaced by a toggle lever which swings downwards and stays in position till partially raised again. A third method uses a lever pivoted between the centre and the side of the loom, the outer end of the lever being hooked under a projection to hold it down, and the shaft up. This system has the advantage that the levers can be selected like the keys of a piano, and all depressed together in one movement.

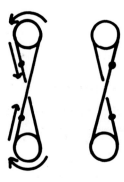

8 *Two shaft roller harness*

a (ii) On larger looms it is more satisfactory to have a cord at each end of the shaft to prevent it rocking and so jamming in the grooves, or giving a lop sided shed. These cords can be operated by a single vertical couper, or be joined to a common knob or common lever. There is no great difference in the mechanical efficiency or in the ease of adjustment of the three systems. An advantage of couper mounting is that the shed can be adjusted for level independent of the amount of lift; with the common knob or lever the amount of lift is fixed, and only the adjustment for level and warp line can, or need, be made. The control is best at the centre, where the shafts can be operated by either hand for speed and ease of weaving, or, failing this, at one side where one hand can do all the work.

A single couper or jack is placed vertically and a cord led to a knob at the side to operate it.

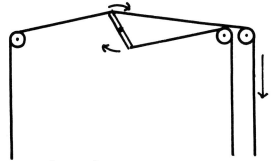

9 *Single vertical couper*

Two cords are taken from the ends of the shafts and joined at a common knob.

10 *Two cords to a side knob*

Similar but worked by a central lever.

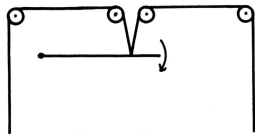

11 *Two cords to a central lever*

Two coupers replace the cords.

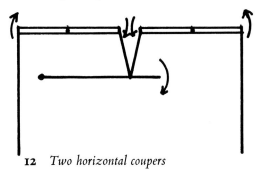

12 *Two horizontal coupers*

There are obviously many variations of detail in the design of table loom mountings, but this covers the main principles.

a (iii) A sinking shed is occasionally used, springs providing the lift at the end of the shafts and a transverse lever the downward movement.

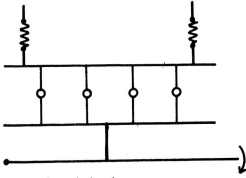

13 *Sinking shed with springs*

2 Foot power looms—rising shed

Rising shed mountings for foot power looms are broadly similar to those of table looms.

a (i) The plain central lift is provided by a single horizontal couper, the pivot being offset to make the action lighter.

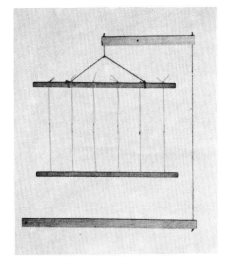

14 *Single horizontal couper*

a (ii) The vertical couper gives an even lift at the ends and the mechanical disadvantage of the march can be offset by lengthening the upper arm of the couper (*15*).

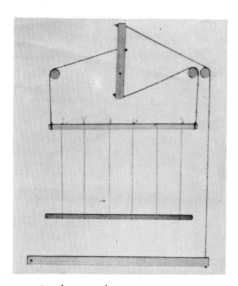

15 *Single vertical couper*

b This arrangement of double coupers gives an even lift and a better mechanical leverage, the treadles having a greater sweep, but needing less effort. The cord running through the warp does not cause trouble if properly positioned, though it can cause fluffing if out of line.

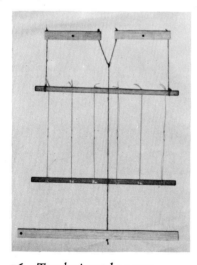

16 *Two horizontal coupers*

c All of the systems need either weights or springs to return the shafts against the friction of the warp threads. Weights have the advantage that the returning tension is constant until the shed is closed, whilst the springs give their greatest tension when it is least needed, i.e. when the shed is fully open, and are almost fully contracted when needed to pull the threads down to the shuttle race. The elasticity of the

warp threads will half close almost any shed, it is the final part of the movement which needs the assistance. There is also the weight of the various levers and friction of the pulleys to be overcome.

3   Foot power looms—rising and sinking sheds

a A more positive method of sinking the threads is to add a set of counter marches pivoted above the marches of a rising shed mounting, and tied to the lower heddle sticks of the harness. Either the loom has to be made 10–15 cm (5–6 in.) higher to accommodate the set of counter-marches, or two sets are interleaved on the same spindle, making it less easy to differentiate between the risers and sinkers when tying up. These however are minor drawbacks when compared with the very great advantage of being able to adjust accurately the amount of movement of each shaft on each treadle.

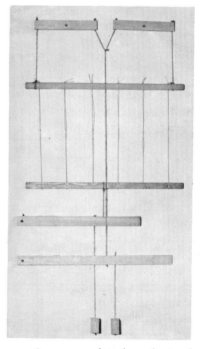

17 *Counter marches above the marches*

b A less complex mounting is the counter-balanced, in which the sinking of one or more shafts provides the lift for the remainder. The shafts are coupled

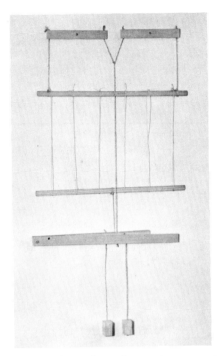

18 *Counter marches and marches on the same spindle*

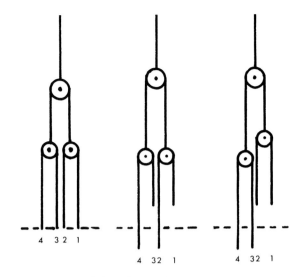

19 *Counter balanced mounting*
20 *Counter balanced mounting, one of each pair sunk*
21 *Counter balanced mounting, one pair sunk*

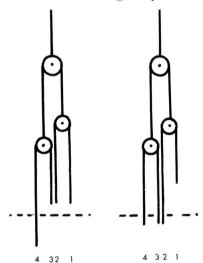

22 *Counter balanced mounting, one shaft sunk, low shed*
23 *Counter balanced mounting, three shafts sunk, high shed*

together in pairs, so that when the one of a pair sinks it raises the other. The pairs are similarly coupled so that when a pair sinks the other pair rises.

The main drawback of this system is that the different types of shed occur at different levels. On sheds in which only one shaft sinks the whole shed is low, and when three shafts are sunk the shed is high. The low shed is usually too small to pass the shuttle, and the high one is so far above the race that the shuttle falls through the warp when the loom is adjusted for normal working. When weaving a whole length of warp faced or weft faced cloth, the batten can be lowered or raised respectively to correct these tendencies. Only a balanced weave (e.g. plain, two and two twill, hopsack, and the traditional overshot) gives a shed with an equal rise and fall. The weaves with mixed sheds (e.g. honeycomb, canvas and mock-leno) are very difficult to weave on this type of mounting unless it is modified. Its advantage is that it does give all possible sheds on a four shaft harness in a mechanically simple way.

The earliest form of counter balanced mounting used heddle horses, and they are still fitted to simple four shaft looms used for limited weaves, as they are cheap and easy to make and maintain. Pulleys are more versatile, and usually more use than horses, except for certain mountings explained in 4. Rollers are less sensitive to unskilled handling than either horses or pulleys, having the advantage of keeping the sheds even, despite warps being badly tensioned or off-centre in the loom. They are not as useful as pulleys when fitting up any of the special mountings referred to later.

A combination of horses and pulleys can be used on harnesses of up to eight shafts, thus avoiding the need for three sets of pulleys and the greater height necessary for them.

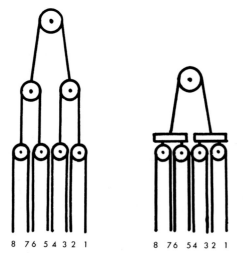

8 76 5 4 3 2 1   8 76 54 32 1

24 *Counter balanced mounting, eight shaft with pulleys*
25 *Counter balanced mounting, eight shaft with pulleys and horses*

4 Special purpose mountings

Most of these mountings require far less cording and adjusting than the counter-march mountings, and whilst not quite as efficient as the latter, they are better than the plain counter balanced mounting. Instead of the one mounting being used for all weaves, these special mountings are used for one weave only. They depend for their efficiency either on reducing the number of sheds obtainable to the minimum for any particular weave, or on using pulleys to give different ratios of movement between the various shafts.

If the top pulley of a counter balanced mounting is dispensed with, and the horses, pulleys or rollers tied directly to the topcastle, the harness is immediately incapable of producing any but four of the balanced sheds. 1 and 2 work in opposition, as do 3 and 4, and of four possible sheds, two give plain weave 1 and 3, 2 and 4, and two give hopsack, 1 and 4, 2 and 3, on a straight threading. As there is no top pulley to even out the lift between the rising shafts, the back pair of shafts can be made to rise and fall further than the front pair to obtain a good shed.

With an odd number of shafts, or a mounting in which differential movement is needed between shafts, an occasional pulley is used upside down, so that it is raised by pulling on the cord which runs over the sheave. This raises the pulley half the distance that the cord is raised, and, conversely, by lowering the pulley, the cord is dropped twice the distance. In actual practice, the cord is usually led up over a fixed pulley and down again, so that one shaft sinking raises another pair or group of shafts by half the amount that it sinks itself, or vice versa.

a (i) The shafts work in the usual pairs over the lower pulleys, and the top pulley is dispensed with.

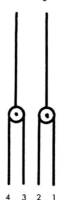

4   3   2   1

26 *Special purpose mounting, plain or hopsack pulleys*

a (ii) The coupers from shaft 1 are tied to the upper heddle stick of shaft 2, and vice versa, the sinking tie only tied (27).

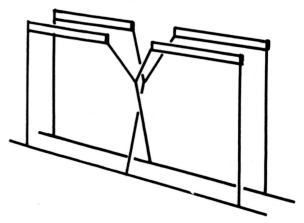

27 *Special purpose mounting, plain or hopsack coupers*

b (i) As for *a (i)*, except that the shafts are paired 1–3, 2–4 as these are the shafts that work in opposition in the $\frac{2}{2}$ twill.

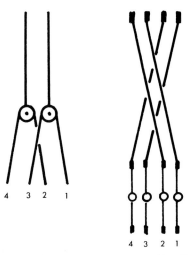

28 *Special purpose mounting, twill pulleys.*
29 *Special purpose mounting, twill coupers*

b (ii) As *a (ii)*, but paired as in *b (i)*.
c Two pairs of horses are used each side, and work in opposite directions. This stabilizes the shed. They can be coupled as in *a (i)* and *b (i)* for $\frac{1}{1}$, and $\frac{2}{2}$ twill, as well as for the full counter balanced mounting.

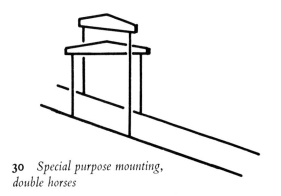

30 *Special purpose mounting, double horses*

d (i) The standard three shaft counter balanced mounting which gives an equal shed on all three combinations for a warp faced and a weft faced twill. The double pulley is made by tying two line pulleys back to back by the bar between the sides.
d (ii) A five-shaft version of the same mounting, which gives an equal shed on all five combinations for any of the five-end twills or satins.
(e) This mounting is for flush spot (or 'Bronson' weave), and distorted weft fabrics. Half the ends are on shaft 1, and the remainder are divided in varying proportions between shafts 2, 3 and 4, either with

spots on all three, or with the ground on shaft 2, and the spots on shafts 3 and 4. The usual pattern sheds are 1 and 2, 1 and 3, and 1 and 4, and though the ratio of movement on these is not quite the same as on the plain weave treadles, it is sufficiently near to cause no trouble. If any two of the back three shafts are to sink, a centre treadle should be used for this shed, and a cord tied from it to the remaining shaft of the three via a pulley on the top castle to give the shaft sufficient lift. The treadle must be down to the floor for this shed, and the extra cord balanced against the two to the other two shafts. Shaft 1 rises easily.

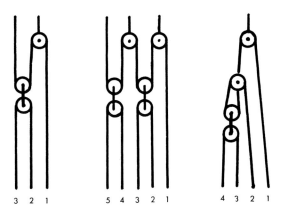

31 *Special purpose mounting, three shaft counter balanced*
32 *Special purpose mounting, five shaft counter balanced*
33 *Special purpose mounting, flush spot, four shaft*

f A five shaft flush spot harness. The cord from the top of the double pulley, up to the top and down to shaft 1 gives the plain sheds, i.e. 1, and 2, 3, 4, 5. The rest of the mounting provides for any three of the back four shafts to sink, and raise the remaining two by an equal amount.

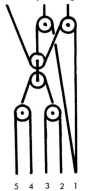

34 *Special purpose mounting, flush spot, five shaft*

g A modification for huckaback The original top pulleys are turned to face forwards, and are replaced in the mounting by line pulleys, which are tied to the top castle by a long loop of cord. This gives the $\frac{1}{3}$ sheds as usual. A cord joins the two line pulleys via the original top pulleys and the new ones, and from this a second cord runs down to an extra march added in the middle and tied to sink with both of the plain sheds (1 and 3, 2 and 4). This raises the whole harness on these sheds, and gives a good lift for the plain weave.

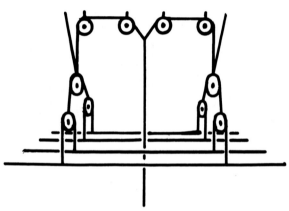

35 *Modification for huckaback*

h Crossed weaves A gauze and leno harness has four shafts, two plain ones at the back, and then, spaced an inch or two away, a pair of shafts combined to give the crossing movement. The front shaft carries a half heddle or doup, which is threaded through the eye of the heddle on the second shaft if it is wire, or is run through the top doup and back through the eye if it is string. More shafts may be added to the back of the harness for more complex crossing weaves or for stripes of plain and gauze combined. On the crossed shed the crossing warp has to be slackened and a moveable bar at the rear of the loom swings forward on this shed to let off enough warp to ease the strain on the threads. This easer bar or slackener works on the upper warp roller. For the operation of the gauze harness see pages 92–5.

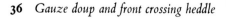

36 *Gauze doup and front crossing heddle*

j Compound mounting A compound shaft mounting is used for patterns in blocks based on damask, double plain cloth, and double faced twill. The compound draw monture is similar, but has a greater pattern capacity. The harnesses, usually two, are set one behind the other, and the warp is entered twice, first in the pattern harness and then in the ground. The pattern harness has the usual small eyed heddles, and the ground harness long eyed heddles, with a 11.5-cm (4½-in.) eye. The treadles work on one harness only, one set making the pattern and the other the ground weave. The only requirement apart from the number of shafts, is a space between the two harnesses. For the operation of the harness see page 89.

k Damask harness This is the name given to a harness which is in two halves, the warp being threaded in sections on one half or the other, to produce check patterns of alternating warp faced and weft faced twill or satin weaves. The two halves work in opposition; when one shaft of the front half is raised, all but one of the back half are raised, and if the first shaft of the front half is the one that is raised, the last shaft of the back ones will be the one that is sunk. The first and last shafts of the whole harness can therefore be coupled over a single pulley, as they will never be both up or both down. The second and the last but one will be coupled similarly and so on. To economise in space, pulleys of increasing size are mounted in a vertical row between two long triangular pieces of wood, the pair nearest the centre using the lowest pulley. The top pulleys are often in pairs as one single pulley would be inconveniently large.

37 *Damask harness*

5 Extra fittings

a Double warp roller This usually added above the warp with a second back beam which can be raised for putting in the warp, and brought down for weaving. Double pawls on the ratchet are a necessity to balance the tension of the two warps. The second roller is used for vertically striped fabrics in which the stripes are of different weaves and therefore different take-ups, for extra warp designs, for fabrics such as seersucker which need different tensions, and for gauze and leno fabrics.

38 *Loom with upper (second) warp roller and easer bar*

b Easer bar This usually operates on the upper roller for gauze weaving. The crossing ends run under the upper back beam, behind the easer bar, and forward to the upper roller. When the bar swings forward and downwards, the crossing warp is given about 7–8 cm (3 in.) of slack.

c Fly shuttle For cloths over 1 m (42 in.) reed width the fly shuttle is essential, but below this a skilfully used hand thrown shuttle is as quick and gives more control over the weft. The fly shuttle is sent out of the box by a leather or leather faced wooden pick, which is returned beyond the back of the box for the next pick by a spring. Up to four shuttle boxes can be placed at both sides of the loom, and any pair can be brought into line with the shuttle race, each shuttle having its own pair of boxes between which it works. By careful planning of the order of wefting, it is possible to use seven different shuttles with four boxes each

side, by constantly picking from alternate sides, but whilst this is easy on a power loom it is hardly worth the effort on a hand loom. The drop boxes are raised and lowered by the hand holding the batten.

39 *Fly shuttle loom with three shuttle drop box*

Additional equipment

1 Warping

a Board or frame The minimum equipment required for a simple warp is one double peg, to carry the cross, and one single peg to take the other end of the warp. A large warp would need a double peg for the portée cross and a treble for the porrey cross.

For warps longer than 1 or 2 m (3 or 6 ft) a frame about 1 m (3 ft) square or a stout board 3 m × ½ m (10 ft × 1 ft 6 in.) is used to carry the pegs for the crosses and other pegs round which the warp may be wound backwards and forwards to obtain the required length. Although the warping board is a little slower to use than the mill, it keeps the warp at a better tension. As the successive turns of warp are laid on the mill one on top of the other the diameter increases, and the last turns are always longer than the first, unless considerable care is taken; while on a board, the last portée is the same length as the first.

b Mill A mill is a skeleton cylinder or drum,

usually, but not necessarily, vertical, and revolving on its longitudinal axis. The number of sides is from four upwards, depending on the size of the mill. A small mill is usually 2 m (2 yds) in circumference, and of either four or eight sides, the latter being better as it permits easier and finer adjustment for the length of warp. The horizontal bars carrying the pegs can be moved from one vertical section to another, and in the four sided mill either the three pegs are offset or one is movable so that a length less than the side, i.e. 0.5-m ($\frac{1}{2}$-yd), can be obtained. The working length of the drum is usually about 1.5 m (5 ft), giving a total possible length of 15–20 m (15–20 yd) for a warp wound in a fairly close spiral upon it. The difficulty lies in keeping the turns of the warp sufficiently compact to prevent their becoming mixed together, and yet not so thick that the last threads to go on are appreciably longer than the inner ones which took a shorter path. A spreader and regulator solves this problem, firstly by laying each turn exactly on top of the previous one, and secondly by providing for the adjustment of the height of the starting point of each layer so that the building up never becomes great enough to be troublesome.

40 *Warping mill and spool rack*

The small vertical drum on top of the spindle of the main drum revolves with it, and winds up or lets out the cord. This raises or lowers the heck block, through which the threads run, and so lays the warp in an even spiral up and down the mill. The adjusting pulley to which the end of the cord is fastened can be locked in any one of about twenty positions, taking up more or less of the cord round its circumference, and altering the starting height of the heck block. The circumference of the adjusting pulley is equal to the distance between two turns of warp on the mill, so that the whole surface of the mill can be used for a wide warp with the threads spread in a thin layer, rather than built up in a series of ridges to the detriment of the tension.

The heck block carries two small shafts of heddles sliding in grooves and a pair of vertical guide rollers. The warp threads are entered in the heddles and run between the guide rollers onto the mill (method of use page 33).

2   Spool rack

A spool rack is a vertical frame having several iron rods onto which the spools or cheeses of yarn are placed, and from which they unwind for warping or bobbin winding. An improvement to the usual commercial rack can be made by screwing eight self-threading guide eyes or screw eyes to the top bar of the frame so that the warp threads can be led up through them onto the mill. A row of eyes, or two staggered rows is useful for picking up a cross by hand instead of using a heck or paddle.

A spool rack for cops has in addition to the rods, a rack at the base with a number of short spikes standing up, onto which the cops are placed for warping.

3   Floor rice

This has two revolving drums which can be set at varying distances apart to accommodate skeins of different lengths. It is by far the most satisfactory piece of equipment for holding skeins whilst they are being used.

4   Doubling stand

This is not often seen, but is a useful piece of equipment. The spool on the bracket half way up stands on a short tube, and the yarn from the bottom spool or spools runs up through the tube and the centre of the upper spool. As the yarns are wound off, the top yarn twists loosely round the bottom one.

5 Bobbin winder

The type of gearing invariably used today is the worm and worm wheel. The worm is of steel, and is turned on the end of the spindle; the worm wheel is of brass. The use of two different metals is to prevent excessive wear on the two gears, but as there is a sliding movement between the gears they need to be kept well greased (not oiled). For this reason the open type is usually to be preferred, those with the enclosed gears being difficult to keep greased.

41 *Rice, doubling stand, and spool rack with guide eyes and cop rack at the base*

6 Threading frame

There are two types of threading frame, one hangs on the wall and the other stands on a table. The back beam of the loom with the warp wound on it is placed in the back of the frame, the shafts on the front and the entering of the warp through the heddles and reed can be done in greater comfort and so at a greater speed. An added advantage for colleges and schools, where space and apparatus are often both limited, is that by using two or three sets of harness and warp rollers, the dead time when a loom is standing idle is cut to a minimum, a student with a warp already entered on a threading frame can often be weaving within an hour of the previous student finishing a length.

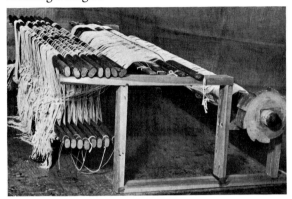

42 *Threading frame*

7 Miscellaneous small equipment (43)

a Shuttles This is probably the most important item of equipment after the loom itself, yet few weavers experiment with the different makes and types to find which suits them best when weaving different types of cloth.

The simple hand thrown shuttle is made with and without rollers underneath, the former having an open bobbin cavity cut right through the shuttle, and the latter a closed cavity which has a floor. The shuttle without rollers is usually longer and finer at the ends and is usually used for very fine work. As it has much of its length in contact with the threads, it will ride over long spaces in the bottom layer of threads without bouncing. If a roller shuttle is thrown through such a shed, e.g. in a large traditional overshot weave, the threads at the far edges of the gaps cause the shuttle to bounce when the roller reaches them. If the top shed is even slightly split, this causes mistakes in the weave. In the simpler weaves the bottom layer of threads is evenly spread over the whole width of the cloth, so no bouncing occurs.

Most of the shuttles of this type are far too light for easy weaving; the older hand shuttles were often drilled and filled with lead plugs to give the extra weight. The light shuttle slows down rapidly with the friction of the warp threads, and consequently needs a very fast and hard throw to make sure of reaching the other side. Even a low shed or a few threads stuck together with fluff will stop it completely. The heavy shuttle on the other hand has so much more momentum, that it rides steadily through the shed at a more even pace, parting any obstruction, and does not require half the initial effort to throw it. The fact that it is heavier to pick up does not mean that it is harder work using it. A 225 g (8 oz) heavy hand shuttle without rollers and with a pirn fitting is the most generally useful shuttle.

A fly shuttle can be anything up to $\frac{1}{2}$ m (18 in.) long, and can weigh 2–3 kg ($4\frac{1}{2}$–7 lb). The nose is armoured with a polished steel point, and there are small inserts of metal on the shoulders where the shuttle rubs on the reed. The rollers have metal bearings which are adjustable and the roller axles are inclined together slightly so that the shuttle tends to run in a curve away from the weaver to ensure a good contact with the reed throughout the width of the loom. There are two or three small porcelain eyes near to the main eye of the shuttle, and by threading the weft in and out of one or more eyes, extra tension can be applied to it. With a strong tension a tenterhook or temple would be needed to keep the cloth out to its full width.

Hand shuttles can be obtained with two bobbin cavities in line, so that a double weft can be used for hopsack etc. without twisting the two threads together, and without other tension difficulties that can occur when winding two threads together.

For rigid heddle and table looms the small roller or closed cavity shuttles can be used, but the stick shuttles are generally of more use. They are made of plywood and have a deep notch in each end. They should not have too much weft wound on, as they quickly become too thick to pass easily through the shed.

b *Reed* The reed, for spacing the warp and beating up the weft, is made of thin strips of metal, known as wires, set edgeways between two pairs of half round rods, and bound into place and spaced apart by one or more turns of tarred twine between each pair of wires. The main dimensions of the reed are its

length, the number of spaces, called dents, to 10 cm or 1 in., and the depth between the baulks, the top and bottom rods. The sett of a reed, i.e. the number of dents to 10 cm or 1 in., is always stamped on the end heavy wire. The useful setts are 10 or 15 (3 or 4) for rugs, and 20 up to 40 (6 up to 10) for general use. It is better to double dent or treble dent in a coarse reed than single dent in a finer one for most purposes. The rustless reeds are far better than the plain ones, unless a reed is in constant use.

c *Raddle* The raddle is for spacing the warp before winding onto the loom. It consists of wooden pegs or metal pins set into a heavy smooth base. As with reeds, raddles are of varying setts. There are also raddles with special setts.

d *Reed hook and threading hook* The reed hook is broad but thin, so that it may pass between the wires of the reed, but is easy to hold and use. The hook itself is fairly large, as it may have to take up to four threads at a time, and pick them up quickly. The automatic reed hook picks up the next wire to the left on the forward stroke, the wire slips down the side of the central moveable tongue which has the hook on it, and then past the end of the tongue. On the backward stroke, the wire has to pass up to the right of the tongue because of the bend to the left at its base, and emerges on the right of the tongue. The right hand wire cannot be picked up because of the bend to the left at the top of the U-shaped holder. The whole hook can of course be turned over to work towards the right instead.

The threading hook for threading heddles is fine, with a small hook, and is set in a wooden handle. The hook has a small opening, so that it will not catch accidentally on the eyes of the heddles.

e *Paddle* This is for warping several threads at once, when a warping board or mill without a heck is being used. It is made of hard wood, about 4 cm ($1\frac{1}{2}$ in.) wide, 5 mm ($\frac{1}{4}$ in.) thick, and any convenient length from 10–20 cm (4–8 in.). It has two rows of holes, which are 2 cm ($\frac{3}{4}$ in.) apart, with about 2.5 cm (1 in.) between the rows. The edges of the holes must be smoothed off, and there must be no rough places anywhere on the paddle.

f *Sticks* There are several different sorts of sticks, but they should all be made of a close-grained knot free wood. The shaft sticks for carrying string

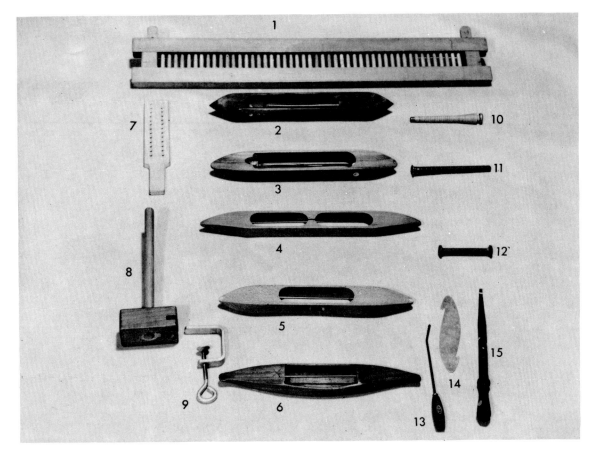

43 *Miscellaneous small equipment*

heddles are thick, and have a half round top and bottom to prevent undue wear of the heddles. The cross sticks are broad, oval in cross section, and have pointed ends like small shuttles. Both cross sticks and shaft sticks have a small hole drilled in each end for the retaining cords.

The back and front sticks for attaching the warp to the warp and cloth beams are both thick, and do not have the holes at the ends.

Warp laths are thin, as they do not take any real strain, their purpose being to stop the layers of warp bedding into each other.

g Rug beater This is a heavy brass or lead loaded wooden fork, with a handle, and is used for beating up the weft in rug weaving on a frame, or on a loom when working in areas.

key

	1	Raddle
	2	Fly shuttle
	3	Heavy hand shuttle
	4	Double bobbin shuttle
	5	Roller shuttle
	6	Hand shuttle
	7	Paddle
8 and	9	Warping post and clamp
10 and	11	Pirns
	12	Bobbin
	13	Threading hook
	14	Reed hook
	15	Automatic reed hook

Warp preparation

a The winding of the warp threads of the correct length and number for a particular piece of cloth is called warping. The threads must all be of the same length and tension, and must be laid so that they do not tangle. To do this the packages of yarn must be placed so that the threads can all be unwound steadily and evenly, and provision must be made for maintaining the order in which the threads are placed initially. The guide eyes and wires on a spool or a cop rack and eyes in the paddle or in the heck, as well as being the means of keeping the threads in order, all provide a slight resistance which helps to maintain an even tension. On a small warp the tension has to be controlled by the fingers.

Cops or cones are better for warping than cheeses or spools, as they unwind over the end instead of rotating. If a large and a small cheese are used at the same time the thread from the larger cheese will be stretched as the movement is started and the greater weight has to be rotated, and will be slack as the movement stops, and the momentum of the larger spool is greater. A number of small warp bobbins can be wound, with a bobbin winder, onto the cardboard tubes from the middle of cheeses or spools. As these are much lighter than the commercially wound packages, there is no great difference between the full and almost empty bobbins, and the tension is fairly even. When yarn is suitable the warp bobbins can be cop-wound and unwind from the end.

All movement in warping must be made steadily, and must begin and end gradually to avoid irregularities in tension. If a warping mill is started quickly the threads are stretched, and if stopped quickly they become slack. This would result in alternate groups of threads being tight and slack at both ends of the warp however even they were in the centre.

b Length of warp The length of warp required is calculated quite simply for most weaves when the length to be woven does not exceed 15 m (15 yd) or so. Weaves which have a large take-up in length

because of high distortion of the threads, e.g. gauze, honeycomb, are dealt with separately in Section III and if a considerable length, 50 m (60 yd) or more is being woven, the simple calculation would not be accurate enough.

As a cloth is woven the warp threads bend round the weft, the two sets of threads displacing each other from the centre of the cloth. This causes the threads to take up in length, and whilst the weft takes care of itself this take-up must be allowed for in the warp. In addition the cloth loses length and width in the finishing. A woollen will shrink, and a hard yarn such as linen will take on a greater distortion. An allowance of ten per cent for take-up and shrinkage combined for all fibres is easy to work out and sufficiently accurate for the shorter warps, and weaves without a high distortion. If anything it gives too great a length on some types of cloth, which is not a serious error.

In addition, the allowance has to be made for the wastage on the loom, which varies from $\frac{1}{2}$ m ($\frac{1}{2}$ yd) on a table loom to $\frac{3}{4}$ m ($\frac{3}{4}$ yd) on a foot power, or more when twelve or sixteen shafts are being used.

c The warp The final warp length will therefore be, cloth length plus 10 per cent, plus $\frac{1}{2}$–$\frac{3}{4}$ m ($\frac{1}{2}$–$\frac{3}{4}$ yd).

The threads or 'ends' of warp are kept in order by crossing them alternately upwards and downwards between two sticks. This cross is essential for maintaining the ends in order before entering in the harness and also afterwards for ensuring that the warp ends reach the eyes of the heddles running parallel and without tangles. The length of warp between the heddles and cross sticks is called the porrey, and this single thread cross is, therefore, the porrey cross.

If the porrey cross were used to spread the warp out to its full width to winding on, the cross sticks would have to be worked down the whole length of the warp, and the careful tensioning on the mill would be ruined by any slight snag or fluffing of the warp. A second cross is therefore made at the other end of the warp, and has four or more ends running together in each direction. This coarser cross is quicker to spread out, and much easier to work down the warp than the porrey cross. As one coarse cross will be made each time the warp is carried down and back, it is called the portée cross, from the French 'to carry'. When making a large warp at least four warp bobbins will be used at once, the ends running together down the mill through the portée cross and back up again, so each portée cross will have at least eight threads.

For convenience in keeping count of the number of threads warped, the ends of a strong yarn of a contrasting colour are crossed between groups of portées, usually the number which makes up 5 or 10 cm (2 or 4 in.) of warp, in the middle of the portée cross. If each knot equals 10 cm (4 in.) of warp width a 90-cm (36-in.) warp would have nine knots, plus one extra portée for selvedges. This is far easier than trying to count and keep track of 728 individual threads at the porrey cross. When checking the number of portées warped the thumbs are placed on the ends of the pegs to prevent the threads slipping off, and the forefingers hold the two upper parts of the cross. By raising the left and right fingers alternately one half-portée at a time can be released.

45 *Counting portées*

d Tying the crosses When the warp is complete, and the threads fastened at the porrey cross where they started, both crosses have to be tied so that the warp can be removed from the mill without losing them. A strong string or twine can be used, or even the threads from all the bobbins together, as is common practice in industry. About 50 cm (18 in.) is needed for each loop, to facilitate the subsequent picking up of the crosses. A small tight loop, besides being difficult to pick up, causes broken threads, incorrect picking up, and fraying of warp ends. At the portée cross one string is threaded away from the warper through one half of the cross by one peg and then back towards the warper through the other half of the cross by the second peg. Then the porrey cross is tied in the same way. The end loop of the warp at the porrey cross must be tied as well, with a shorter string following the peg at the end. If this is not done, the upper and lower layers of the end half of the cross will come apart, and the porrey cross is lost completely. The loop of the portée cross is usually tied in the same way to save time and trouble in picking it up later, though this tie is not essential.

44 *Counting knots of warp at the portée cross*

46 *Crosses and end loops tied in warp*

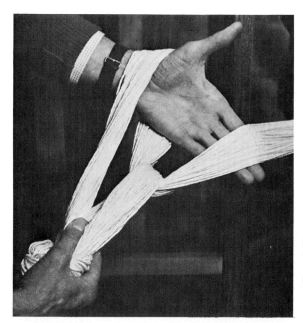

47 *Chaining warp 1*

The warp is removed from the mill by chaining it from the porrey cross, so that the portée cross, which is to be used first for winding the warp onto the loom, is at the end of the chain which will undo easily. It is better to tie a loop in the beginning of the warp, and then make the chain through this loop, than to pull the warp through its end loop. If the chain knot becomes twisted, it is easier to undo this end loop and unchain from the wrong end than unchain either by pulling the whole warp through each knot of the chain or pushing the raddle through. Ties should not be put round the warp in various places before chaining as is sometimes done. They serve no useful purpose, as the chaining holds the warp together sufficiently, and when a tied part of the warp approaches the raddle, the tie prevents the threads from moving past each other slightly, with a consequent tightening of the selvedges and slackening of the centre.

The warp is always begun at the porrey cross and finished at the same place. This avoids having loose half portées at the raddle, and knots in the threads on the warp beam. The knots at the beginning and end are cut off in any case before threading and cause no trouble.

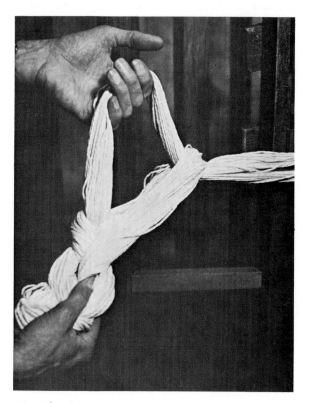

48 *Chaining warp 2*

1 Warping

a (i) *Post and clamps* The length of warp is measured along the edge of a table, and a single post clamped at one end and a double post at the other, allowing about 2.5 cm (1 in.) to the m (yd) for stretch. The thread is tied round the single post in a loop about 5 cm (2 in.) long, and the thread taken down to the double posts, round the end and back again between the posts, and up to the single post. This completes two threads and makes one cross. This is continued until the total number of threads required has been warped, when the thread is tied off at the single post again, with a 5-cm (2-in.) loop as before. Both these loops are included in the string when the end of the warp is tied prior to its removal from the pegs. The cross is tied as for the portée cross, and as it serves for both the portée and porrey crosses the warp is chained from the single post. A warp of this type is usually quite small, so that stripes of different colours are set in by breaking off the first colour and tying the new thread to the old thread, *not* round the warping post. As long as this knot is within 5 cm (2 in.) of the post, it will cause no trouble in subsequent operations; it will be either cut off at the single post end or be too near the warp roller to be amongst the heddles if at the double post end.

a (ii) A small warp on a *frame or a board* is treated similarly, the only difference being that the warp is taken backwards and forwards between several pegs on the frame or board to make up the length in a more compact and convenient way.

A large warp is dealt with in the same way as a warp on a mill. The portée and porrey crosses are usually arranged to come near the centre top edge of a warping board, for convenience, and this is sometimes possible on a warping frame. If not, the porrey cross is at the top left-hand corner of the frame, and the portée cross at the bottom right.

49 *Warping board showing the arrangement of the crosses*

Care must be taken to lay the threads on the pegs without overlapping; it is better to put successive portées on with a slight space between each, and

then push them down to the base of the pegs when the pegs are full.

b *The warping mill* The threads are tied together, and put half under and half over the left-hand peg of a set of three at the top of the mill; after the porrey cross has been taken they are led down to the right in a fairly flat spiral to the lower set of pegs for the portée cross. A steep spiral makes the threads on two sides of the cross different lengths. Allowance should be made when fixing the bottom pegs for the stretch which will occur in warps laid on by hand, or wound from large cheeses; 2.5 cm to the m (1 in. to the yd) is sufficient. The second half-portée is laid on top of the first, and the whole warp should be laid neatly, otherwise the turns of the spiral merge into each other, and it is easy to put on one turn too few or too many. If the warp is building up too much, it can be taken off, the whole warp being completed in two or three sections. It is also simpler to handle a warp during raddling and winding on if it is in sections of no more than 30 cm (12 in.) wide.

c *The porrey and portée crosses* The smallest number of bobbins that can be used for warping is four, and it is also a convenient number for many of the traditional tweeds and colour and weave effects. The four spools are placed on the rack with the thread unwinding from the underneath so that the lower threads will clear the upper spools.

c (i) The threads are led through the eyes on the rack, threaded alternately through the eyes of the back and front heddles of the heck, brought through the guide rollers, and finally tied together and placed over the left-hand peg of the set of three at the top of the mill. The cross is taken, and the mill rotated to the left until the bottom set of three pegs is reached, starting and stopping slowly to maintain an even tension on the threads.

The four threads are taken down between the first two pegs, round the end and down again between the same two pegs (*50*). The mill is then rotated to the right.

When near the top the front heddle is raised to give the first half of the cross, which is placed above and below the right peg (*51*).

The back heddle raised by the third and fourth fingers, so that the thumb and first finger can take the top half of the cross. The left hand is brought forward with the right from this position and the second half of the cross is placed on the middle peg (*52*).

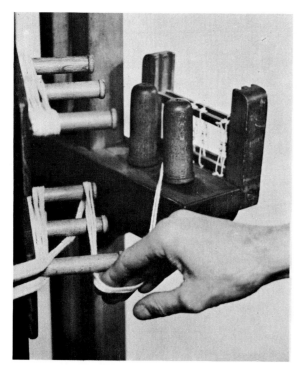

50 *Warping   1 portée cross*

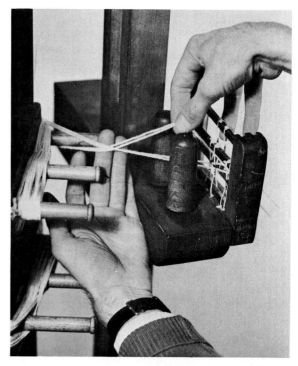

52 *Warping   3 porrey cross, upwards, second half*

51 *Warping   2 porrey cross, upwards, first half*

53 *Warping   4 round the end peg*

The four threads are taken together round the left peg (53).

The front heddle raised for the first half of the cross again on the middle peg (54).

54 *Warping   5 porrey cross, downwards, first half*

The back heddle raised for the second half, which is shown completed and on the pegs (55). When this is finished, the mill is given sufficient momentum to the left to enable the weight of the heck block to continue the rotation, and immediately the previous portée is marked up.

An alternative method is to take the whole of the second cross on the thumb and fingers of the right hand and place it on the pegs complete. This is useful when making a warp for certain colour and weave effects for which the second cross has to be turned over before it is placed on the pegs.

The porrey cross at the end of the previous portée has been taken, and the four threads have been brought round the end. The nearer heddle frame of the heck (white threads) has already been lifted and the threads picked up on the back of the thumb. The far heddle frame is raised with the third and fourth

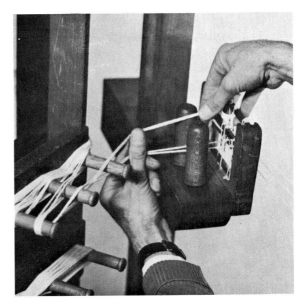

55 *Warping   6 porrey cross, downwards, second half*

fingers, and the second finger inserted into the cross from the far side (56).

56 *Taking the porrey cross in the hand to turn over   1*

The right hand is brought over to the pegs, downwards to catch the black threads on the centre peg, and then in towards the pegs to put the white threads under the centre peg and the second half of the cross onto the right-hand peg (57).

57 *Taking the porrey cross in the hand to turn over* 2

c (ii) An equally efficient way of controlling the threads and taking the porrey cross is to use a paddle. This is a piece of hard wood with two rows of holes 2.5–4 cm (1–1½ in.) apart, and 2 cm (¾ in.) between the holes. The warp threads are brought through the holes in regular order from the spool rack, tied together and placed over the left-hand peg. The first porrey cross is taken and then the threads gathered together between the right thumb and forefinger, while the paddle is held in the heel of the hand by the third and fourth fingers and the ball of the thumb. The threads are taken down to the right, through the portée cross, and back up the mill to the top set of pegs. The paddle is transferred to the left thumb and forefinger, and the threads are held by the other three fingers, so that the right hand can take the cross.

58 *Paddle*

The thumb is put between threads 1 and 2. The first two fingers go below the far thread and pull it up towards the warper, the hand turning over slightly, palm downwards.

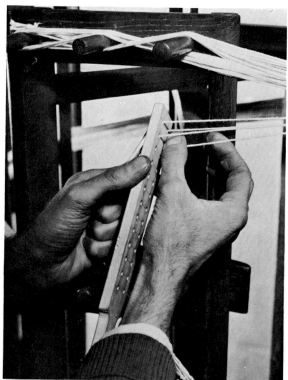

59 *Warping with the paddle* 1 taking the first thread

The first two fingers go over the near thread and press it downwards, the hand turning back to its original position (60). Threads 1 and 2 are now crossed, the cross being held by the thumb and two fingers.

The same movements are repeated, and the paddle moved to the left so that the part of the cross on the thumb can be placed on the centre peg and the two fingers parted to put the remainder of the cross on the right-hand peg (61).

The paddle is taken round the end peg and transferred to the right hand, *without twisting it*. The handle of the paddle faces downwards towards the warper at all times, and never goes over the threads. The left hand movements are similar to those of the right hand, except that as the first thread has become the nearer one of the pair when the paddle was turned round the end peg, it is now pushed down instead of being pulled up. It is pulled up when coming up the mill, and goes down when going down the mill.

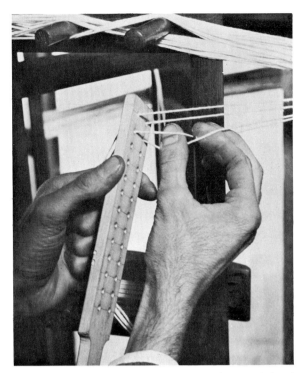

60 *Warping with the paddle   2 taking the second thread*

61 *Warping with the paddle   3 putting on the porrey cross*

The thumb is between threads 1 and 2, the hand has been turned slightly palm down, and the first and second fingers have pressed the first thread down.

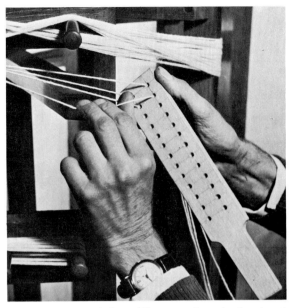

62 *Warping with the paddle   4 taking the first thread*

The two fingers have lifted the far thread and the hand has turned back again.

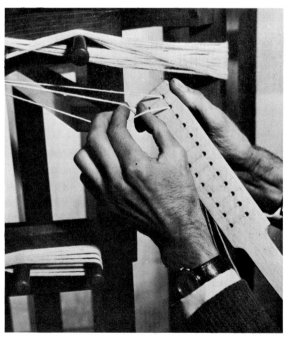

63 *Warping with the paddle   5 taking the second thread*

The second pair of threads has been picked up and the cross placed on the centre and right-hand pegs as before.

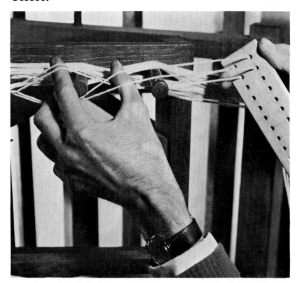

64 *Warping with the paddle   6 putting on the pottery cross*

With only four threads on the paddle, it is possible to take the cross correctly, place the part held by the fingers on the peg, and then allow the paddle to hang vertically and try to place the pair of threads on the same side of the paddle onto the other peg instead of the pair across the top of the paddle. This can be rather confusing at first, but as the mistake cannot be made with six or more threads in the paddle it is as well to practise taking the cross with six threads on the paddle before making a warp, threading six 1 m (1 yd) lengths of strong yarn through the paddle, tying them together at each end, and hooking them over any convenient peg to give them the necessary tension.

c (*iii*)   If the spool rack has two rows of guide eyes along the top, the porrey cross can be taken as on the paddle, except that all four fingers have to be used together because of the length of the rack compared with the paddle.

c (*iv*)   A warp can be made with a single cheese of yarn, and still have a portée cross. The porrey cross is made as usual, but at the portée cross the yarn is passed down between pegs 1 and 2, round 3 and then up between 1 and 2 instead of down, laying both threads in the same direction. This is repeated once or twice more, giving 4 or 6 ends in the half cross.

The next half cross is made in the same way, but the threads go up between 1 and 2, round 3 and back down between 1 and 2.

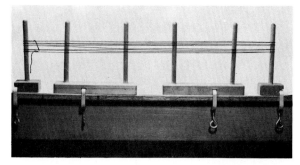

65   *Four thread portée cross, warping with a single thread*

d   Multi-coloured warps   The sizes and proportions of the stripes in warps for colour and weave, checked, and striped fabrics vary so much that it is unwise to be dogmatic about the way that they should be done. Generally speaking the colour and weave fabrics can be warped with one repeat of the colour to a half-portée, the only difficulty being to keep the colouring plan in order at the porrey cross when turning round to go down the mill. Wide stripes and pin stripes or overchecks are often better warped with one warp for each colour and the warp mixed on the raddle.

d (*i*)   *Large stripes*   The total number of warp ends of each colour is calculated, as well as the number in each stripe. The number of bobbins used for warping will depend on the width of the stripe, as half-portées cannot be split in the raddle. The number of bobbins should divide exactly into the number of ends per stripe. If this is impossible, and the proportion is so critical that the width of the stripe cannot be adjusted by a few threads, the next half-portée above the number needed must be completed, and wound on the loom, the spare threads being dropped out in the threading. If the colour changes are infrequent each stripe can be tied off at the top when finished, and the heck rethreaded for the next colour. If a paddle is being used, each colour can be kept threaded in its own paddle, and the change is easily made.

d (*ii*)   *Small stripes*   These are found in colour and weave designs, such as basket weave, dogtooth etc.; and are usually warped in one or occasionally two warps.

One and one colouring is threaded in the heck or paddle in the usual manner, the one colour being on one shaft of the heck, or one side of the paddle. The porrey cross when coming up the mill is taken normally, but the one going down has to be turned over to bring the colouring plan right. It is no use taking the wrong shaft of the heck or the wrong thread of the pair in the paddle before the correct one, as this does not alter the order of colouring, but makes two double threads appear in the cross between the two half-portées.

Two and two colouring is easier than one and one if it is threaded correctly. The obvious way of threading LLDD would necessitate reversing the cross as for one and one colouring; if it is threaded LDDL, and the taking of crosses done as for a plain warp, the last thread of one half-portée pairs with the first of the next half-portée, e.g. LDDL, LDDL. The odd thread that this leaves at each side of the warp can easily be worked into the selvedge.

Four and four colouring is warped as for two and two, with the one colour in the centre and the other at the edge of the half-portée (see also *d* (*iv*)).

Colouring plans which are not symmetrical such as a 1–3 or a 2–1–1 are warped as the 1–1, with the downward porrey cross turned over. The portée cross is, of course, unaffected by any difference in colouring plan.

d (*iii*) *Fine lines and overchecks* These present no difficulties. The warp for the line is made separately from the main warp, often from a single bobbin, and then set in the raddle after the main warp. One thread of the main warp is dropped out and a thread from the line warp substituted where required.

d (*iv*) *Mixtures* There are two types of warp stripe which do not fit into any of the previous sections, the gun club check, and the compound stripe on a plain ground.

The gun club check is coloured 4–4–4–4, with the second and fourth groups being the same colour, i.e. L, M, D, M. For this two warps would be made, one for the whole of the main colour (M), and the other a 4–4 colouring for the two other colours. A better way would be to use sixteen bobbins, and warp as a one and one, turning the downward porrey cross over, but the only feasible way to do this is to wind warp cops, and make a cop rack with four inch nails or screws, as has been done on the spool rack shown on page 27.

A similar method to that for the gun club check is used for the second type of warp. One warp is used for all the ground colour, and a second and possibly a third is used for the stripe. If the compound stripe is fairly narrow, warp cops can be wound for it, otherwise it will be warped in sections and brought together in the raddle.

e Sectional warp beam A sectional warp beam is a built-up skeleton beam, with a circumference of usually 1 m (1 yd). It is set with small pegs at 5-cm (2-in.) intervals along its length. The correct number of bobbins for 5 cm (2 in.) of warp is set up on the spool rack, and the threads tied to the first section of the beam, which is then rotated the number of times required for the warp. A porrey cross is taken, the threads cut and tied off, and the same process is repeated with the second 5-cm (2-in.) section, each section of warp lying between two rows of pegs on the beam. It is an excellent and speedy method of warping, provided that sufficient work is being done to justify its use. The main drawback is the large number of warp bobbins required, which in turn necessitates either a considerable quantity of yarn, or the accurate winding of bobbins.

2 Raddling or spreading

Before touching the warp, the cross sticks and back stick from the loom are prepared. A length of fine loom cord, or twine, about 30 cm (12 in.) longer than the stick is tied through the hole at one end of each stick with a clove hitch round the cord itself. A similar cord is tied with a clove hitch and bow to one end of the back stick.

The two loops of string through the cross are held in one hand and the string through the end loop in the other (66). When these are pulled apart it is easy to find the end loop of warp. The back stick is put through the loop and the cross sticks either side of the cross. The cords are now tied to the ends of their respective sticks, with the same knots. The two sticks should *not* be tied together, as they would be difficult to move down the warp.

A peg to which the warp can be tied is clamped to the far side of the table, and the raddle put into the block to hold it. The raddle should be such that the warp is about 10 per cent wider on the beam than the reed width, so that the warp tapers from back to front. This gives less wear on the selvedge threads, and keeps them running firmly.

If no available raddle will take the warp in even numbers of portée per dent, it is possible, for ex-

66 *Picking up the portée cross*

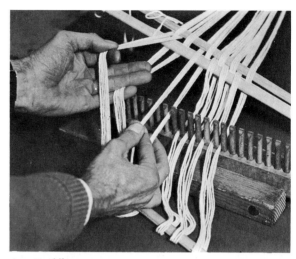

67 *Raddling*

ample, to dent 2, 3, 2, 3 half-portées or 2, 2, 2, 3 for 8 and 7 ends per cm (20 and 18 ends per in.) respectively when using four bobbins for warping, and an 8 dents/10 cm (2 dents/in.) raddle. If the raddle is moved across the loom and back whilst beaming, and the selvedges watched carefully, the slight irregularity causes no trouble on warps up to 10 or 15 m (10 or 15 yd). If much work is done at a sett which involves this sort of irregular denting, it is worth having a raddle made to a sett which will take an even number of half-portées per dent. One such raddle has seven dents to 10 cm (4 in.), and takes one portée per dent when warping with four bobbins, to give $5\frac{1}{2}$ ends per cm (14 ends per in.) on the warp beam.

a The warp is next tied with a clove hitch onto the peg, the back stick being 4–5 cm (1–2 in.) from the edge of the table. The cross is untied and is worked down until it is about 30 cm (1 ft) from the end of the warp, and in this position the cross sticks are lightly tied together, running the string in a figure-of-eight round the sticks, to prevent them overlapping; the strings just removed from the cross serve this purpose well.

When denting an even number of half-portées per

dent, pair them with the half over the near cross-stick as the second one of the pair. This one is much easier to pick up, and when moved to the right takes the previous half-portée with it. It makes the work much quicker, and is worth doing, even when it means having an odd half-portée at the end of the warp and splitting up the portées between the dents of the raddle.

Through the whole of the raddling, keep the left hand and the warp threads as low as possible to avoid lifting the sticks and therefore the threads high enough to come out of the raddle. If this makes the operation difficult, a piece of stiff paper or thin card about 10 cm (4 in.) square can be folded in two and placed on the teeth of the raddle; the unused warp rests on this before being threaded.

When the raddling has been completed, replace the cap and tie or peg it on securely immediately. The strings originally used for tying the cross can be removed from the cross sticks and be used again for tying the cap on the raddle.

b A reed may be used instead of a raddle, a whole portée being pulled through a dent, and the next few dents missed. For example, if the final threading is to be two ends per dent, a whole eight thread portée would occupy four dents of the reed, so the threading for raddling would be, thread one, miss three. Every fifth portée would be, thread one, miss four. This would give the necessary 10 per cent extra width to the warp on the warp beam.

The method of threading a reed as a raddle substitute is the same as that for the preliminary threading of a rigid heddle, and is given (see page 107). At the end of winding onto the loom both the portée and porrey crosses will be in front of the reed, and will have to be transferred to the back of the reed before it can be removed for threading. This is also similar to the rigid heddle process described in Section IV following the preliminary threading.

c Two or more warps The striped warps present no difficulty in raddling, the main warp is put in first, leaving the necessary spaces for the other threads. If two warps only are being used, they can be wound onto the loom with two sets of cross sticks in them. With three or more warps it is better to pick up all the warps on one pair of cross sticks. When the second warp is in, the two cross sticks nearer the raddle, one in each warp, are raised or turned on edge. A third stick, or better still a 15-mm ($\frac{1}{2}$-in.) diameter rod with a pointed end, is worked through the shed formed in the upper warp, and the groups of threads from the upper part of the shed in the lower warp are picked up over the stick between the appropriate groups of the bottom shed in the upper warp. If an assistant holds the original cross sticks, this process is

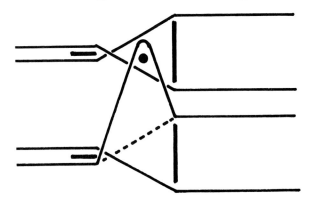

68 *Transferring crosses from two warps on to one pair of sticks*

quite straightforward. The second half of the cross is done in a similar way, and when the two new cross sticks are tied in, the four original ones are taken out. The same process is done again for each successive warp added.

The fine warp for the overcheck or pin-stripe can be left on its own cross sticks. It needs to be on top of the main warp for easy threading, so it is raddled first if the warp is to be wound on from the back of the loom, or second if wound on from the front.

3 Beaming or winding on

This is usually done from the front of the loom, after the harness has been removed. If the previous tie-up is no longer required, the marches and counter marches can be disconnected, and the shafts placed on the top castle out of the way. If the tie-up is needed again, the whole harness and mounting can be lifted down from the top of the loom, complete with the couper frame on a counter march loom, and rested on the treadles. The upper shaft sticks should be tied together before moving them to save tangling with the heddles. If two lengths of loom cord are tied to the back beam and stretched to the front uprights of the loom, the raddle and the cross sticks can be rested on them; the retaining cords of the cross sticks can be undone and retied to include these cords, so that the sticks can still slide, but cannot fall off. The cords should *not* run through the end dents of the raddle, as the raddle must be moved slightly from side to side whilst winding on the warp. Alternatively, the raddle can be supported from the top of the loom to hang in line with the back beam.

a (i) The warp is spread evenly on the back stick by turning the stick round two or three times each way while pulling on the warp, the raddle meanwhile being held firmly. The centre of the warp should now coincide with the centre of the back stick, and the middle cord from the warp beam is tied round the middle of the back stick. As the back stick is now held by the centre, there is no possibility of the stick twisting sideways and tangling with the warp. The two ties nearest the selvedge are added next, and finally any other ties are added on the left and right alternately. If there are four ties from the warp beam, a temporary tie can quickly be put round the back stick and back beam of the loom to hold the stick until the outer ties are on. (See pages 60-1).

a (ii) If the loom has a cane roller the warp rod is placed in the groove, the second rod brought down inside the warp and into the groove to hold the first in place and a full turn carefully made.

The warp can be wound on from the back of the loom if space permits. This saves dropping the harness and mounting on a foot power loom, and moving the heddles or removing the shafts on a table loom. The process is more or less the same, the only real difference being that the raddle now stands on the weaving bench or stool, or on two chairs at the back of the loom, or in its block on the table for a table loom.

b Tensioning methods The absolute essential for good weaving is good tension in warp and weft. Good warp tension begins on the warping mill or board and though a badly made warp cannot be greatly improved, in the beaming a well made warp can be ruined if badly beamed.

If the warp has been well stretched whilst turning the back stick to spread and centre it, the tension of the half-portées will be equal on both sides of the loops. One full turn should now be wound onto the beam, so that the threads can no longer slip. If the sticks are worked down the warp before this is done any slight snag will cause the half-portée in which it occurs to move down with the sticks, and pull the other half-portée up towards the back of the loom, with the consequent upsetting of tension. If the cords of the lacing of the beam, or ties of the apron cause the tension to vary slightly, a round of half a dozen warp laths should be wound on with this first turn. A cane roller will not present this problem.

A heavy and even tension should be applied to the warp whilst beaming it. The warp should be held centrally with both hands together as far away from the loom as is practicable, and at least 3 m (3 yd). The distance from the hands to the centre of the raddle is less than the distance from the hands to the edges, so if the warp is held firmly but too near to the raddle the centre becomes slack as the warp is wound on. This can be overcome by holding the warp in one hand with the thumb uppermost, the thumb being pressed firmly on the centre, and the sides being permitted to creep slightly past the thumb. This requires considerable practice to do it accurately and is more suitable for a table loom. The warp should never be divided into two parts and held by right and left hands separately, as the pull is never even with the two arms, and the weaker arm will give a slacker half warp and cause considerable trouble in the weaving as well as a slightly curved length of cloth.

Another method of beaming is to put on from half to one turn, depending on the type of warp, and then pull roughly equal sections of the warp (about 10 cm (4 in.)) strongly. This makes the beam fairly firm, and it is easy to keep the tension even if done from alternate sides. It has the advantage of making beaming possible single-handed.

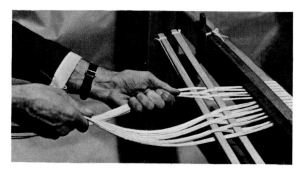

69 *Tensioning a warp in sections*

If beaming has to be done in a very confined space the warp can be brought forward over the breast beam, back over the knee beam, down under the cloth beam and finally upwards and forward. This gives a longer length with which to work, and the extra friction gives a higher tension.

As long as the beam feels firm to the touch and the selvedges have not spread far, laths are not necessary. A slight amount of tapering at the selvedges is not harmful; it keeps the selvedge ends working tightly, but when the tapering becomes too pronounced it will cause overtightening and breaking of the selvedge ends. On a loom with a 10-cm (4-in.) diameter warp beam this should not occur for 2 or 3 m (2 or 3 yd), and when it does a round of laths must be put in to give a new firm surface to the whole beam. The space between the laths should not be big enough to allow the threads over them to touch the previous layer of warp, but as few sticks as possible should be used. Putting in one stick here and there as the warp is wound on is useless, as it causes constant variation in the selvedge tension.

A round of thin card the full width of the beam may be wound in to prevent successive layers of warp cutting into each other, but a card flexible enough to do this will not be firm enough to hold the selvedges out. Paper is of little use as it is too thin to prevent groups of threads cutting into the softer parts of the beam.

Selvedge papers can be used to keep the diameter built up at the edges, and this saves using laths if the warp is strongly tensioned. They are made by folding a strip about 15 mm ($\frac{1}{2}$ in.) wide down the length of a piece of stiff paper, and refolding five or six times more to give a strip several layers thick down the length of the paper. This is curved by pulling it firmly over the breast beam or a similar edge, and is then wound into the warp with the thick layer just outside the last thread of the warp, preventing the threads from slipping outwards, and counteracting the taper on the previous layers. An A2 420 × 594 mm (half imperial 15 × 22 in.) sheet of cartridge paper (drawing paper) is excellent for this purpose.

When the warp has been wound to within 1–1½ m (3–4 ft) of the end, the porrey cross is picked up on two more sticks, and worked up the warp for 20–30 cm (8–12 in.) or so, as it is more easily done now than later. If the cross is difficult to move, the lower half should be pulled a few threads at a time diagonally outwards and downwards from the upper threads.

Although the work of the portée cross is now finished, it is as well to keep it until the threading of the heddles is completed, as it provides a quick check on the number of threads used, and often, as in the case of a straight threading, a check on the accuracy of the threading as well.

The cross sticks in the porrey cross should be fastened behind the shafts on the cords previously used to hold the portée cross sticks, and the harness returned to its normal position, for threading. The breast, knee and cloth beams are now removed ready for entering the warp ends into the heddles.

4 Threading or entering

The warp ends are cut off above the tie through the end loop. This ensures that all the ends are cut; if the loop of warp is cut instead, tight ends are often missed and cutting them later slows down the entering. As soon as the ends are cut, they are tied into a bow (see page 68) to prevent tangling, and the possibility of losing the cross. Before starting the actual entering, the number of heddles per shaft should be checked from the draft. Straight-forward threadings are simple, but irregular threadings should have the number of ends per shaft for one repeat of the pattern carefully worked out, and multiplied by the number of repeats. If any of the shafts is short of heddles they are more easily added, or transferred from shafts with a surplus, now rather than later when the warp has been partly threaded. Any shafts which still have too many heddles should have the

spare ones left roughly equally on either side of the warp, particularly when using wire heddles. On a table loom used for its full width, about 10 spares is all that can be left on each shaft, as otherwise they rub and wear the selvedge threads.

In all the processes which follow, it is assumed that the work is commenced at the extreme right of the warp, and continued steadily through to the left. Unless two people are working on the same loom together, there is nothing to be gained by working from the centre outwards. The time saved in not counting heddles is more than offset by working left handed on half of the warp. A bunch of ends from the right-hand side sufficient for 5 or 6 cm (2 or 3 in.) of warp is brought to the left of the heddles needed for them on each shaft, and tied round with a larks head in a piece of thick cotton warp yarn or tape. On a table loom this is tied to the cloth roller, on a foot power loom to a piece of string round the weaver's waist. Keeping the warp ends stretched facilitates the selection of the correct thread from the cross for entering into the heddles and later the reed.

a (i) A bunch of warp ends is tied on the left, and the left hand encircles a group of heddles on all three shafts. The right hand pulls the first heddle from the group, and then, while the left hand finds the eye of the heddle, takes the first warp end from the cross and brings it well forward to give plenty of slack. The thread is held across the top of the first finger by the thumb. The left thumb is placed into the eye of the heddle and pulls it down to the left to open it to a triangular shape.

The right forefinger presses the thread through the eye of the heddle, pulling the right side of the eye gently to the right to open it, the left hand steadying the other side.

The right thumb now slides along the side of the top joint of the forefinger, from the nail to the knuckle, rolling the loop of warp thread over the side of the eye, and then pinching it between the side of the top thumb joint and forefinger (*72*).

The loop of warp is drawn through the eye to the full extent of the slack, which should be sufficient to bring the end through as well. The somewhat awkward movement of the thumb sideways shows here.

The heddle is slid to the right, and the sequence is repeated, taking the heddles from the different shafts as required for the pattern.

70 *Threading string heddles   1 pulling out the thread and holding the eye*

72 *Threading string heddles   3 drawing the thread through*

71 *Threading string heddles   2 inserting the entering thread in eye*

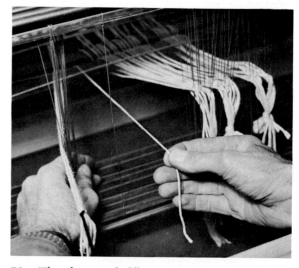

73 *Threading wire heddles   1 drawing out the thread*

a (*ii*) Wire heddles are threaded in a similar way. The bunch of warp threads is tied as usual, the left hand placed round the heddles. The warp end is brought forward as before.

The last three fingers of the right hand are taken up to the right over the warp thread and down again, so that the warp comes up over the back of the first finger and down between it and the thumb (*74*).

The second finger slides the thread up over the end of the first finger so that it slips into the groove between the finger and thumb. A slight pull with the right hand brings the loop of thread into the groove.

The thumb is slid back down the finger, and the loop stands up slightly away from the finger. The loop is then threaded through the eye of the heddle, the finger and thumb opening slightly as it goes through (*75*). The threading is rather like threading a large eyed darning needle with thick wool after having made a tight loop over the needle.

74 *Threading wire heddles   2 making a loop*

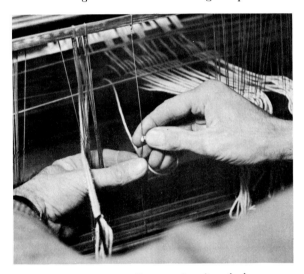

75 *Threading wire heddles   3 threading the loop*

The finger is pressed against the back of the eye while the thumb brushes the loop sideways (76).

The thread is drawn through, and the heddle moved to the right.

If more than four or five shafts are being used, they are divided into groups of three, four or five, according to the weave, and each group held in turn.

This method of threading heddles will give a threading rate of five hundred or more an hour with practice, and though slow at first is worth mastering.

If an assistant is available, a threading hook can be used. The bunch of warp threads is tied, and the left hand holds the heddles in the same way, the left hand

76 *Threading wire heddles   4 drawing the loop through*

selects the heddle, and the right hand inserts the hook and pushes it well through *upside down*. The assistant can put the loop of thread under the hook and pull it upwards much more easily than the opposite, as the warp and cross sticks are in the way of a downward movement. The hook is pulled back, pressing slightly upwards against the top of the eye of the heddle to prevent the heddle being caught in the hook.

When several repeats of threading have been completed, or the bunch of threads used up, the threading is checked for accuracy. A straight threading on four shafts with a warp made with four bobbins will use a half-portée to a repeat, so a quick check to see if the repeats and half-portées coincide is all that is necessary at this stage. The warp ends are then tied in a bow, and the whole group pushed over to the right.

Selvedges are threaded according to the types of yarn being used. A soft yarn needs a double thread through each heddle for the first 5–6 mm (¼ in.) of cloth; a fine hard yarn is set singly in the heddles, but is doubled in the reed. This means that the first 5–6 mm (¼ in.) of cloth is either of a doubled thread at the same sett, or a single thread at twice the sett. The selvedge can, with advantage, be eased into the body of the cloth by missing one dent between them.

b   Threading the reed or sleying   Except when using coarse threads, and particularly cotton threads, it is not advisable to use one dent of the reed for one thread. In a plain weave the warp ends are spaced the thickness of a pick of weft apart, or slightly more. If the reed wire is no thicker than this space the cloth will weave easily, though a tweed warp may fluff a little. In a twill or similar weave where only each pair of threads is separated by a pick of weft, the threads are set more closely. Each reed wire would now have a space equivalent to half the thickness of the weft yarn if dented similarly, so the denting in the reed should be two ends per dent on a reed half the sett, i.e. two ends per dent in a 65/10 (8s) reed for sixty-five ends to 10 cm (16 ends to 1 in.).

77 *Cross section of plain weave and 2/2 twill or similar weave*

On a fine cloth, even in plain weave, the wires are obviously too thick to set the warp singly or even double, and three or four ends per dent are frequently used to prevent crowding of the warp and fluffing and sticking together of the warp ends. Evenly irregular denting, such as 1–2–1–2 or 2–3–2–3 can be used to obtain setts between single and double, or double and treble denting if the reed of the right sett is not available.

The reed is best threaded in the horizontal position. It should be tied with two or three loops of string from the top castle to hang roughly in line with the lower shaft sticks. Before threading, the width of the warp and the length of the reed should be compared, and sufficient space left at the right-hand end to bring the warp, when finished, in the centre of the reed.

To make selection of the warp ends easier when a complicated threading or a large number of shafts or a high sett is being used, the shafts can be raised by hand and two cross sticks put into the plain weave (or the nearest to plain weave that is possible), in front of the shafts. Selection from this cross is easier than selection from between the heddles.

b (i) Bunches of warp ends are tied as for threading the heddles and brought over the reed.

The reed hook is inserted in the reed from underneath, with the hook proper pointing towards the heddles and the first finger of the left hand selects the first thread from the first bunch of heddles threaded.

The thumb goes inside the thread, and the second finger grips the thread against the side of the thumb.

78 *Threading the reed   1 taking the first thread*

The hand is turned over slightly, and the length of thread between the thumb and forefinger hooked downwards through the reed.

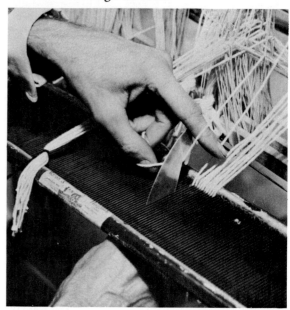

79 *Threading the reed   2 hooking the thread through*

46

b (*ii*)   The automatic reed hook is used in the same way. Care must be taken to pull the hook vertically downwards, or it will 'break' as it passes through the reed. It must be pressed slightly to the left on both the upward and downward movements to make sure that the next dent is picked up correctly.

b (*iii*)   A quick and accurate method of threading the reed is to use sley knives, which are boxwood or bone reed hooks thick enough to stick in the reed. They are used in pairs. As one is used and the thread pulled through, it is put in the next dent but one, as the second knife is already in the next dent. The knife is put in sloping upwards towards the weaver, and the lower end of the knife already in the reed is knocked towards the weaver at the same time so that the upper hooked end is then pointing towards the heddles ready for the next thread. In this way it is impossible to miss a dent or double up, and it is no slower than using the plain reed hook.

5   Tying on

Before attempting to tie any part of the warp, the threads must be well worked down with the fingers, (not combed) to remove any twists and inequalities of tension from the porrey. Heddles must be approximately in the correct place, so that the warp is in line, through the harness and reed, and the harness must be checked quickly for height and level. If it is already well below the warp line, and is to remain so for the weaving, it is as well to tie a loop of string round the shafts at each end and hang them temporarily from the topcastle; otherwise the group of threads which first take the weight of the lower part of the harness will be badly slack when the other groups are tied and share the strain.

The warp is divided into bunches of not more than 8 cm (3 in.) of reed width, and 5 cm (2 in.) at the selvedge. If wider bunches are tied, there is a comparatively large difference between the length of centre and edge threads of each bunch when the reed is brought up on the first few picks. Either the edge threads are stretched and the first part of the weaving spoiled, or more warp is wasted than is really necessary. If much smaller bunches are used, there are more tensions than need be to equalise, and the work of tying on is made more difficult. Only the beginning of each knot is made when first tying the bunches of warp threads onto the front stick. The centre bunch is tied first to hold out the front stick, then the selvedges are added. The remaining bunches are tied in order, working from the centre outwards and taking a bunch alternately from left and right of the centre to keep the warp balanced. By the time that the selvedge has been reached, the centre will be slack, and starting again at the centre, each bunch is re-tightened and the knot completed. As the final bunches are the two selvedges, slackness, if any, will be in the centre of the warp, where it will cause least trouble. Often the selvedge bunches can, with advantage, be slightly overtightened, and they should in any case be kept well out to counteract the tendency of the threads to pull into the centre of the knot; in fact in most warps the centre of the selvedge knot can be in line with the first thread in the reed.

When this has been completed, run the hand quickly and smoothly once or twice across the porrey, and any slack places will cause the fingers to drop downwards. This is a more accurate way of checking the tension than by patting the warp in front of the reed.

There are two commonly used knots for tying on the warp, as well as several others of more limited use

a   The knot most commonly described is not in fact the most efficient; it is less sensitive when adjusting the tension, and as it pulls the threads together in front of the stick it wastes more warp than is necessary. It is possibly a little easier for a beginner to tie.

A bunch is divided in two, and the two halves taken over the stick and back underneath.

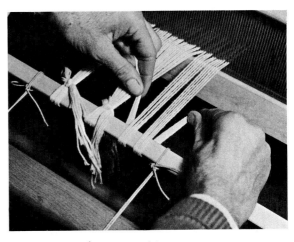

80   *Tying on the warp*   *A1*

The first half of a reef knot is tied in the two ends *(81)*.

81 *Tying on the warp*　*A2*

The reef knot is completed, one end being left through, making a loop to undo the knot easily if necessary *(82)*.

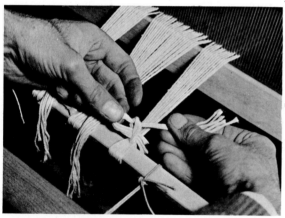

82 *Tying on the warp*　*A3*

The centre knot in the first photograph shows the knot half completed and tightened for the preliminary tying, and the left-hand knot is fully completed.
b The other knot is commenced by taking one half of the bunch over and the other half under the front stick. The end from below the stick is crossed over the end above the stick. If the hands are held as in the photograph, the second finger can hook this (lower) end through twice in quick succession *(83)*.

The end has been tucked through twice. The right hand is never normally in this position; it is so here to demonstrate the formation of the first part of the knot *(84)*.

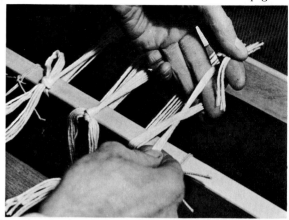

83　*Tying on the warp*　*B1*

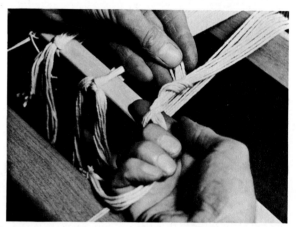

84　*Tying on the warp*　*B2*

The knot is tightened by pulling the upper end towards the weaver with the right hand, and the lower end away from the weaver with the left.

85　*Tying on the warp*　*B3*

◄ *Cushion cover in four-block overshot weave*
See page 84

The left hand is then pulled back firmly capsizing the turns of the knot, and pulling it to the edge of the stick. The centre knot shows this stage completed for the preliminary tying, and the left-hand bunch the finished knot.

86 *Tying on the warp* B4

The end originally from below is held with the left hand and the other end tucked through to make a loop for untying. This is similar to a surgeon's knot.

6 Errors and corrections

WARPING

On the warping mill, if the warp is not made neatly and the turns of the spiral run into each other, a turn too few or too many can be put on. The warp should be chained until the end is reached, and the incorrect threads cut. Extra lengths are tied in, or the surplus is cut off as necessary, and the threads rejoined.

If a half-portée has been missed in the cross, it is raddled in its correct place, determined by the position of the half-portée to which it is attached, and left where it is.

If any of the porrey cross is missed, the threads are best put through the porrey cross sticks by hand, judging the order as far as possible with reference to the portée cross; ensuring that any stripes are in the correct order.

When using the paddle with only four ends through it, the second half of the cross can be put on the peg sideways instead of endways (see page 38) or the whole of the second cross can be put on the wrong way round. In either of these cases, leave the

threads on the sticks, and thread in the correct order as determined by both the crosses together.

If the portée cross is lost completely, stretch the warp on the floor for its full length and trace the portées back from the porrey cross. If the porrey cross is lost, make a new one after tracing the portées down from the portée cross.

If a stripe or a line has been omitted from a warp, the warp can be moved over and the missing stripe is wound on an improvised second warp roller and set in its place. An error in a stripe usually means re-threading to the nearest selvedge.

RADDLING

There is little that can be done other than re-raddle if a dent has been missed or doubled. If the cap of the raddle has not been tied down tightly enough threads can move about into different dents, at first unnoticed. Wind the warp off again until the correct part is reached, re-thread where necessary and continue beaming.

BEAMING

The only real cure for any fault developing during beaming is to go back as far as necessary and rewind the warp. The chief faults are: selvedge threads slipping off the warp laths, warp off centre, tension too slack giving a soft beam which will then cause unevenness in tension in the rest of the warp, and a tight but badly wound beam in which the portées have piled up because the raddle has not been moved from side to side to spread the warp evenly.

THREADING

If a heddle has been missed a new one is tied in, and on a single-coloured warp a new thread set in and weighted to tension it. If the warp is striped in any way, the whole warp has to be re-threaded to the nearest selvedge, except when the weave and the colour repeats are both small, then the remainder of the repeat can be taken out of the heddles and discarded. The same applies in the case of a heddle which has been doubled, the whole repeat is discarded if small, or the warp is re-threaded, or with a plain warp the extra thread cut out and the empty heddle left where it is.

When a pair of threads stay in the centre of the shed, it usually indicates those threads have been crossed in front of the heddles. A single thread staying in the centre of an open shed may be caused by: missing the eye of the heddle completely, in which case it always stays in the centre; threading through the top or bottom doup by mistake for the eye in which case it will shed rather more than the other threads in one direction, and not at all in the other; crossing the threads within the harness, e.g. a thread going to the left instead of the right of the heddle in front of its own heddle, which again sheds well one way, and poorly, with a centre thread, the other. The remedy for all these defects is the same: cut the faulty threads at the knot on the front stick, and withdraw them from the harness and re-thread correctly, then finally tie a short length of similar warp to the ends of the threads and re-tie onto the front stick. This is better than undoing and re-tying a whole bunch of warp ends which have already been correctly tensioned, just for one or two threads.

Any error in the reed, doubling or missing a dent, can be corrected only by re-threading to the nearest selvedge. It is better to remove the threads dent by dent as they are required for re-threading, than take all the threads out and start again.

Loom preparation

1   Theory of shedding

The shed is the space between the two layers of warp threads through which the shuttle passes with the weft. The relative density of the two layers and the sequence of the lifting of the threads are determined by the weave.

The depth of shed needs to be little more than the depth of the shuttle; as long as there is sufficient room for it to run through easily, any further movement of the threads not only strains them unnecessarily, but allows the shuttle to bounce and pick up incorrect threads. The distance from the cloth beam to the warp beam should be as long as is practicable, as any movement of the threads away from the centre line stretches them, but the longer the length of thread to take the strain the less proportionate stretch occurs.

a Tension   The tension of the two layers is usually unequal as a better cover is obtained if the bottom layer is tighter than the top. As the top threads fall and become tight between the rising threads the weft 'kneads' the slack ends centrally between the tight ends, thus helping to break up any reediness caused by denting in twos or threes. This difference in tension is obtained by having the heddle eyes below the centre line if the loom is in the resting position, so that the sinking ends are further from the centre than the rising ends. A back beam higher than the breast beam also helps. On a rising shed mounting the opposite takes place as only the top threads move.

b Differential rise and fall of shafts   The shedding should occur as near as possible to the fell of the cloth so that the actual movement of the threads may be small; the further from the cloth the heddle works, the greater the lift has to be to maintain the same angle.

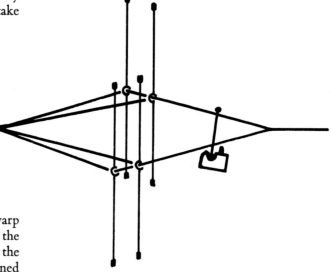

87   *Differential rise and fall of the shafts*

2   Mounting a loom

This is usually taken to mean tying all the cording into both upper and lower mountings.

The shafts should first be made up and hung by loops of cord from the top castle at approximately the correct height. Before placing the string heddles on the sticks a length of fine loom cord or twine is tied firmly to the right-hand end of each stick. The heddles are placed on in their bundles, making sure that both loops are not twisted. When the shaft is complete, the twine is tied to the left-hand end; the knot being 'slipped', i.e. finished with a half bow, so that it may be undone easily if heddles have to be taken on or off the shaft. This retaining cord should always run outside the cords of the mounting looped to the sticks, as only then can heddles be moved along the shafts past the cords of the mounting without undoing the retaining cord or the mounting cord.

String heddles are usually mounted with the knots at the top, as they are then easier to mend or re-tie. If the knots are placed at the bottom any mending or substitution has to be done from underneath. With short heddles (less than 25 cm (10 in.)) it is sometimes better to mount them upside down to prevent the ends of the heddles fouling the threads of the upper shed.

If a considerable number of heddles has to be added to an already stretched harness, it is better to put the old ones on the back shafts, and mount a complete shaft or shafts of new heddles at the front. If some new and therefore shorter heddles are added to an existing shaft, the old ones adjacent to them will be slack and cause bad shedding, and in extreme cases can tangle with the warp threads.

Wire heddles are more trouble to mount as they have to be done singly. New ones will have one end painted, and they should be put on all facing the same way. If an eye is at the wrong angle, the heddle is upside down. When transferring wire heddles from one shaft to another strong threads can be run through the top and bottom eyes with a darning needle, and loops about 8 cm (3 in.) longer than the space occupied by the heddles tied round them. If this loop is held stretched by an assistant, the heddles can be coaxed fairly quickly onto the new shaft.

a (i)   Table looms   On a small table loom the lifting cord can often be tied directly to the centre of the shaft without any great detriment to the shed, but on a wide one a bow cord tied along the shaft helps to give a more even lift. It should be stretched firmly, as there is usually little space to spare between the shafts and the top of the loom. It is best threaded through both holes and tied in a long loop from end to end of the shaft using a span knot. The lifting cord is then cut to length, with a generous allowance for the knots. A figure-of-eight or a thumb knot is

tied in the end, the cord threaded through the knob and the centre hole and tied round both strings of the bow cord together with a round turn and two half hitches, or a variation of the ossel hitch. The toggle lever is threaded from the pivot side as the cord must be able to swing across the pivot to lock the lever in the down position when the shaft is raised.

a (ii)   On a loom with vertical or horizontal coupers the cords to the ends of the shafts are again threaded from the levers towards the shafts, with a figure-of-eight knot at the lever end, and a round turn and two half hitches round the shaft. The cords from the coupers to the knobs should include provision for adjustment near the centre and have figure-of-eight knots at the ends. Snitch knots can be used between the coupers and the shafts if desired. Mountings with two pulleys are also corded from the knob towards the shafts, and can have snitch knots just above the shafts.

b (i)   Foot power looms—rising shed   A rising shed foot power loom with wire healds is very similar to a table loom; the lifting will usually be by witch or dobby, and there will be a double cord with a snitch knot for adjusting the height from the lifting hook to the bow cord.

The bow cord can be single, with a loop at each end to accept the double cord from the shaft in a snitch knot, and it would then be tied to the centre cord with a sheet bend. If it is double a snitch knot need not be used, the lateral adjustment being made by sliding the bow cord through the lark's head which is used on the lower end of the centre cord. The ends of the bow cord are usually tied a quarter of the length of the shaft from each end, and rise to about a half or a third of the distance between the shafts and the top-castle.

A rising shed loom with string heddles is more likely to have a couper lifting system than a mechanical one. The side cords will have a figure-of-eight at the top, and a bowline or a loom harness knot making a loop about 10 or 12 cm (4 or 5 in.) long at the bottom, ending 12 or 15 cm (5 or 6 in.) above the shaft. A double cord is fastened by a lark's head to the upper heddle stick inside the retaining cord and fastened to the loop with a snitch knot. A short cord is run between the inner ends of the coupers, and from this the long, doubled streamer cord, attached by a lark's head, runs down to join the march with a snitch knot. This knot, as with the snitch knots on the treadles, is tied with the loop coming up and the two ends coming down, as it is much easier to hold the weight of the treadle or the march on a loop and pull the two ends through, than do the opposite.

Vertical coupers are joined to the shafts as are horizontal coupers, the streamer cord is also similar, with the snitch knot near the march. If a single thickness of cord is sufficient a loop is made at the lower end as for the cords of the shafts, or better still, a double cord is tied with a sheet bend to the end of the streamer, so that the loop of the snitch knot can be on the march for ease of tying.

The marches are tied to the treadles according to the weave plan, only those of the shafts required to lift being tied for a rising shed mounting. All the treadle cords are cut first, of such a length that the snitch knot will come roughly in the centre of the cord. The ends are joined with a figure-of-eight knot, and if the cord is a little fine for the size of the hole in the treadle a brass washer is threaded on first to prevent the knot pulling through. The loops are threaded up through the treadles, and pulled hard to settle the knot. If the hole is rough or the cord thick, a needle and twine can be passed down, through the loop and up again and the loom cord pulled through by the twine. Loops are put in only where a shaft has to be lifted by a particular treadle, and for efficient working the two sets of holes should be vertically in line. The cords from the marches are cut to give about 10 cm (4 in.) overlap with the loops, have a figure-of-eight tied in the middle, and are threaded down through the holes and joined with a snitch knot to their respective treadles.

b (ii) Foot power looms—rising and sinking shed, counter march action The rising shed of a rising and sinking counter march mounting will be the same as a rising shed mounting. The sinking action is much simpler than the rising action. A double cord is looped over the lower stick with a lark's head, again inside the retaining cord, and is joined by a snitch knot to the counter march.

The marches of the shafts which have to rise, and the counter marches of those which have to sink for any one shed are all tied to the treadle for that shed. The counter marches were usually shorter than the marches, and placed above them on the older looms, but the modern practice is to place them on the same spindle and make them equal in length. This has the

advantage of saving height, but more care is needed in tying. It is easier on the older type to put in the rising ties first, on the long marches, and follow with the sinking ties on the counter marches or short marches, completing one treadle at a time. On the later type it is better to work shaft by shaft down one treadle, tying risers and sinkers as required.

b (iii) Foot power looms—rising and sinking shed, counter balanced action The lower mounting of a counter balanced harness is tied between the lower heddle sticks and the marches in the same way as the sinking action of the counter march mounting. Stability can be improved by using a short spring shaft between the lower heddle stick and the march. It is fastened to the shaft by a double loop of cord with a lark's head at each end, threaded through on the shaft and looped over the end of the spring shaft. The tie to the march goes from the centre of the spring shaft as described above for the shaft. The spring shaft is from a quarter to a third of the length of the shaft, and is rather like an inverted heddle horse. The loops needed are tied with a reef knot round two pegs on the warping mill or two large nails in a block of wood so that they are all of equal length. On this mounting only the sinking ties are made.

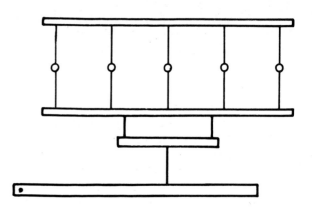

88 *Spring shaft*

The upper mounting may use horses, pulleys or rollers. The heddle horses are attached to the shafts by loops of equal length. The simplest way is to make the loops first as already described for the spring shafts, and put them onto the shafts, tucking one end of the loop through the other and then making the lark's head knot and slipping it onto the end of the heddle horse. With well stretched cord this method

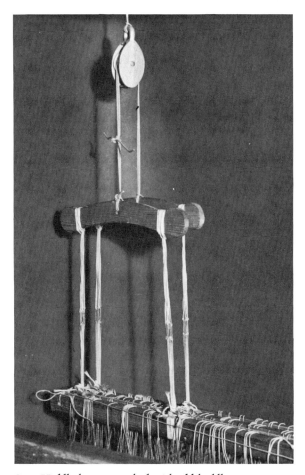

89 *Heddle horses attached with old heddles*

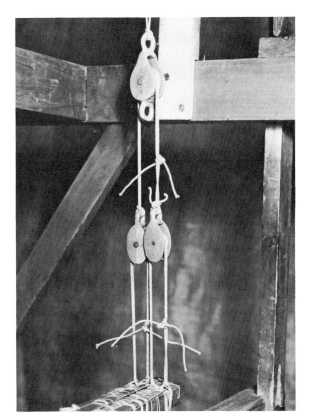

90 *Pulley mounting*

is adequate. Snitch knots can be used instead, if the cord used is inclined to give badly. A quick way of ensuring perfect accuracy is to use half a dozen or so old string heddles that are not fit for further weaving, and loop these on in a bunch instead of the loom cord. The horses should be tied on each shaft equidistant from the centre of resistance, i.e. a shaft should be attached to both outer or both inner ends of the two horses which control it. The horses on either side should also be parallel; if not they can foul each other and give almost no shed.

Pulleys are fastened with a snitch knot in the double cord about four inches above the top shaft. It is generally easier to have the loop on the near shaft and the ends coming from the far shaft, over the pulley and down to the loop. The shaft pulleys are coupled over the top pulley in a similar manner.

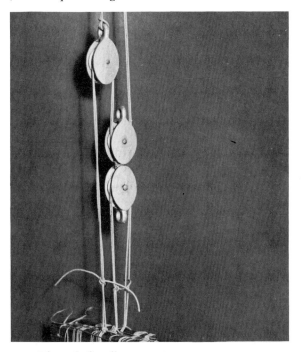

91 *Three shaft pulley mounting*

92　*Roller mounting*

93　*Combined horse and pulley mounting*

Rollers are mounted in a similar manner. The double cord from the far shaft takes a complete turn round the roller before being knotted to the loop. There is a slight increase in steadiness if the cords are both wound either towards (or away from) the centre, rather than both to the left (or right). The upper rollers are treated similarly.

Combined horse and pulley mountings are mounted as in the relevant sections above. The pulleys can be tied or hooked with screw hooks onto the horses.

In all mountings the cords fastened directly to the shafts and running either up or down should be equal to all the others of the same set. The snitch knots where inserted are for maintaining the accuracy of this balance, and not for adjusting the rise or fall of the shafts. Only on the knob or lever table looms, without the bowcord, where there is a single cord from the shaft to the lever does this not apply.

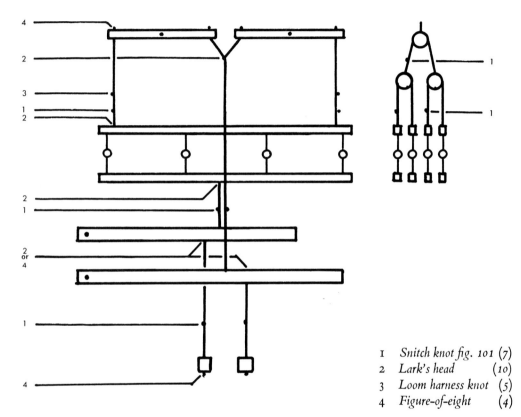

94   *Diagram of a full counter march mounting showing the position of the knots*

1   *Snitch knot fig. 101*   (7)
2   *Lark's head*   (10)
3   *Loom harness knot*   (5)
4   *Figure-of-eight*   (4)

3 Theory of adjustment

A well adjusted loom should not only have a good shed, but should be easy to operate. A loom difficult to work takes up too much of the weaver's attention, and the quality of the cloth suffers in consequence.

The starting point is always the theoretical warp line and the actual warp line is related to this. To even out the top and bottom tension on rising shed looms the warp can be about 15 mm ($\frac{1}{2}$ in.) lower at the heddles on a table loom and up to 4 cm ($1\frac{1}{2}$ in.) lower on a foot power loom, provided that the return weights are heavy enough to maintain the warp at weaving tension. On a table loom this is not usually a practicable proposition except for very narrow warps. On a rising and sinking shed foot power loom about 15–20 mm ($\frac{1}{2}$–$\frac{3}{4}$ in.) is usually ample to obtain the necessary difference in tension for good cover. The actual amount of shed should be just under 5 cm (2 in.) on a table loom, and about one and a half times the depth of the shuttle on a foot power loom. A larger shed on a table loom merely strains both warp and cords, and on a foot power loom under certain conditions it allows shuttle bounce to develop as well. The bottom of the shed should lie firmly on the race, but should not bend over it enough to fray the warp. The various levers, coupers, marches and heddle horses should be set to give the best mechanical advantage, which except for the rising shed vertical couper means truly horizontal, when the shed is fully closed. They should also not foul each other. The cords should be vertical and must be equidistant either side of the centre of resistance. Knots must be tied where they do not interfere with other moving parts of the mounting; snitch knots need extra care, as the long ends can tangle with warp threads or other cords.

a Table looms The actual amount of lift on the simpler table loom is determined by the travel of the lever, or the position of the blocks for the knobs, and cannot be altered. If there is a stop to check the fall of the shaft, the cords can be progressively shorter towards the back of the loom, giving the necessary differential lift on the top shed. As the back shaft needs the greatest lift, set its cord so that the shaft is barely on the stop, then raise the shaft, and adjust the other shafts in order from back to front so that all the sets of warp threads are in line at the reed. If a single cord is being used without the bowcord, it is better not to use the hole drilled in the top bar of the shaft, the cord may then be moved slightly off centre to counteract the tendency of the shaft to stick in the guides if the warp itself is off centre or is slack on one side. On a loom with coupers or side pulleys the lift at each end of the shaft keeps the shaft level at all times whatever the condition of the warp. On these looms the differential lift is usually provided in manufacture by staggering the blocks, or the projections for the levers.

b Foot power looms On a foot power loom with coupers of either type, these are first fixed in the central position. The cords from them down to the shafts are now made equal in length, adjusting the front shaft to the actual warp line, and checking for level across the loom, usually by making the shafts parallel to the batten cap, after checking the adjustment of the latter first. The remaining shafts are levelled in turn, working to the back, the distance of the first and last shafts from the top castle being measured to prevent their being set successively higher as can easily happen when levelling each shaft to the previous one.

Next the marches and counter marches are levelled to the horizontal after the knots have been tightened and stretched by pulling down on the ends of the marches.

Finally the coupers are unpegged and the treadles adjusted. As the weaver's whole weight goes forward when about to throw the shuttle, the treadle should touch the floor when the shed is just fully open. This allows all the extra weight to be taken by the actual treadle straight to the floor, and avoids excessive strain being taken by the mounting, harness and warp threads, with consequent damage to the warp and premature wearing out of heddles.

Adjust the rise and fall of the back shafts first to the required depth of the shed, and then set the others on the same treadle to these levels. The batten should be hung centrally, and can be tied back to the weaving position so that the sinking threads can be resting on the shuttle race without excessive bending. The position of the rising threads should be noted, so that all the treadles give an equal depth of shed. The back shafts will have to rise and fall more than the front to maintain the same angle, so the back cords will be tighter than the front.

On back hung treadles the front ties move more

than the back ones, so on this account too the front ties have to be slacker than the back. On front hung treadles the back ties have the greater range of movement, so that to a certain extent these two factors will then tend to cancel each other.

95 *Counter march loom with front slung treadles and marches and counter marches on a single pivot*

96 *Counter march loom with back slung treadles and marches and counter marches on separate pivots*

The distance of each treadle from the pivot of the marches affects the total amount of movement required; those furthest from the pivot requiring the greatest range, so that when the loom is in the resting position, with the coupers pegged on a counter march action, the treadles will not be level, but will be progressively higher the farther they are from the pivot.

97 *Loom adjusted, showing progressive rise of the treadles to the free end of the marches. Unused marches are tied slightly higher than those in use*

When the treadle is depressed, various parts of the mounting move towards each other or to fixed points of the loom frame, and often this limits the range of movement available, particularly if a loom has been converted from a counter balanced to a counter march mounting, or has had more treadles added.

The lower heddle sticks of the sinking shafts will approach the marches of the rising shafts on the counter balanced mounting, and their own rising marches as well on a counter march loom (*98*). The harness must be set high enough for the shafts to reach the limit of the necessary movement without actually touching the counter marches or marches.

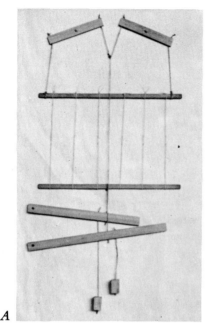

A

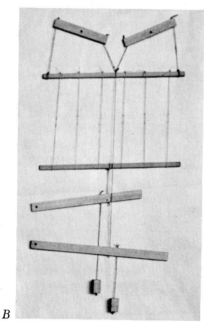

B

98 *A and B. Counter march mounting showing the need for good working clearances. The relative heights of the lower heddle sticks and the counter marches and marches on A sinking and B rising sheds should be noted*

In a similar way the falling marches or counter marches will tend to foul the treadles which are rising as the shed is opened. The worst side is that away from the pivot of the marches, where the treadles have to be set higher initially and the movement of the marches is also greatest. At this side, if the treadles are set too high they will come into contact with the cloth roller as well. The traditional long and short marches in two sets can foul each other on a wide loom unless great care is taken, or the loom is built much higher than is usual today.

If either of the first two working clearances is inadequate, raising the harness will cure the fault on both the counter balanced and counter march looms by giving more room for the march to work. Lowering the harness slightly will often correct the third fault by reducing the actual amount of lift on the rising shafts. If it does not, the only thing to do is to accept the limit on the treadle furthest from the pivot, and balance the whole mounting to give an adequate shed on that treadle. Often the tie-up can be re-organised to give a little used shed to that particular treadle and the others can be given a better shed if it is essential.

c Faults The fault which causes more trouble than anything else is having the warp off centre, particularly in the case of the simple table looms and the counter balanced foot power. Less obvious, but just as troublesome, is having a warp which is slack down one side. A similar fault appears when there are too many wire heddles at one end of a shaft on a table loom.

In an evenly tensioned warp its resistance to the shedding movement is the same right across, and the centre of resistance is the centre of the warp. If the warp is slack down one side, the resistance to being moved will be less on that side, so that the centre of resistance will no longer be the centre of the warp, but will be nearer the tighter side of the warp. If the pull is still applied at the centre of the warp, the side with less resistance (i.e. the slack side), will move more easily, and so open further than the tight side. On a counter balanced foot power loom this will give an uneven shed, deeper on the slack side. On a table loom the consequent turning movement causes the shaft to jam in the groove before the shed really opens. The only cure, apart from re-winding the warp, is to move the cord applying the pull along the shaft until it reaches the centre of resistance, and so gives a level shed.

A warp evenly tensioned but off centre will have exactly the same effect as there will be more threads on one side of the centre than the other, giving a greater resistance on that side.

The cording of the upper mounting on a counter balanced loom of any type of action should also be set equally either side of the centre of resistance to give the best results, using spare pulleys tied to the top castle instead of fixed top pulleys if necessary. Scandinavian built looms often have the top pulleys moveable sideways so that they can be set just outside the selvedges whatever width is being woven, and on such looms the re-spacing of pulleys is easy.

The advantage of using rollers in the upper mounting of a counter balanced loom is that even with an off-balance warp of either sort, the shed will still be reasonably level as the cord at both sides must move by an equal amount. The cords tend to creep under the unequal pull, but it is only a moments work occasionally to correct this. On a well balanced warp they have no advantage over pulleys.

The third fault of this type, that of having too many spare wire heddles on one side of a table loom, is easily dealt with, remove the surplus heddles.

Another fault in mounting common to all types of loom is that of crossing the cords of the mounting. On a table loom the cords from two levers can run to the opposite shafts. On all three upper counter balanced mountings, the cords from two of the shafts can be crossed right round each other and can cause enough friction to give an uneven shed, and the heddle horses can jam because they are pulled together. On a counter march upper mounting the coupers can be fastened to the wrong shaft at one end, and will then give a crossed shed.

The ties between the shafts and the marches or counter marches, or between the latter and the treadles can be crossed, so that the wrong shaft is operated, and a treadle tie can cross sideways as well.

On a counter march loom the rising and sinking ties can be crossed, or one shaft can be tied both to rise and sink at the same time

Faults peculiar to the horses involve the balance of them relative to the centre of the loom. The two cords from the same shaft should be equidistant from the centre, i.e. use both outer or both inner ends of the horses. Otherwise a state of unbalance similar to that of an off centre warp results. The horses on the same side should be parallel, otherwise the ends which touch will often not cross when changing shed. The cords should be vertical, if they slope inwards as they

go down to the shafts, the horses twist horizontally, and again will not cross past each other.

Pulleys give little trouble if kept oiled. The cords can come off the sheave and jam between it and the side of the block, or a wrongly placed snitch knot can stick as it runs through the block and give a smaller movement on that particular shed. A sticking pulley can be freed with a few drops of oil.

Rollers should be kept running parallel, and the sling or screws at the ends should be kept oiled. The cords should be wrapped round in the same direction, i.e. both towards or both away from the front of the loom, and should all work inwards to the centre or vice versa, and not all to the left or all to the right.

The wrong pair of cords can be tied in a snitch knot in a counter march loom mounting, e.g. the two ends of a streamer cord can be tied correctly to the march, and then one of them paired with one of the ends from a lower shaft stick and tied to the counter march or vice versa.

On all parts of looms which have holes for the cords drilled vertically the knot can pull through the hole. If thicker cord is not available a small brass washer can be put on the cord, or a thumb knot tied over the figure-of-eight knot to increase the size of the knot.

Heddles can cause bad shedding as distinct from errors in the weave. A heddle stick, usually a lower one, can go through a heddle on the next shaft, so that particular heddle is drawn down by both shafts. The sheds in which both shafts are tied to sink or rise together work normally, but others fail to give a clear shed. If the retaining cord breaks or becomes undone, the heddles can slip off the shaft stick, again usually the lower one, and will not give the sinking shed. If heddles slip off the heddle stick and onto the retaining cord when the warp is as wide as the shafts are long, those heddles give a smaller sinking shed. If some heddles of the wrong size are added to the harness whilst threading, the longer ones will give a poor shed. The same effect occurs if the eyes in some of the heddles are longer than the others, or if the eyes are set at a different level. Knots in a heddle occasionally slip or come undone. If one of the eye knots slips, the heddle will give a small shed in one direction. If the end knot slips or comes undone, the heddle will shed in one direction only. If the heddles are mounted knots uppermost the fault is obvious immediately from the resulting tangle with the warp.

4 Beams or rollers

The almost universal way now of preventing the warp and cloth beams or rollers from rotating is by pawl and ratchet. The pawl is the moveable pointed tongue which engages with the teeth on the wheel. It is easy to operate and requires no maintenance, but is coarse in the adjustment of tension. As the cloth is woven the warp takes up in length and so tightens itself and affects the beat. If the cloth roller is let off one tooth the warp then becomes too slack. A second pawl can be screwed above the first, to engage a tooth when the first pawl is midway between two teeth. This has the same effect as doubling the number of teeth on the ratchet wheel, and a let off of one half tooth in the weave up will usually correct the tension sufficiently.

A much better method is to have a wooden box the length of the warp beam hung from two ropes which are taken two or three times round the beam and then weighted with small counter weights to keep them tight on the beam. Weights are placed in the box until the warp is at the correct tension, and this is then maintained without variation. Instead of being rigid the warp is now elastic. It gives slightly when shedding and when beating up, and the tension is constant despite the take-up. The quality of cloth is better, and the weaving easier. When the box of weights finally reaches the roller with successive windings on, the counter weights are lifted gently and the box drops to its original position.

A friction brake is used on looms with an automatic take-up. One end of a cord is fastened to the loom frame, and the other is wound two or three times round the beam and then tied to a weighted lever. This allows the warp to unroll as necessary but still maintain an even tension.

There are three methods of attaching the warp to the warp beam, with a cane, with lacing or with an apron.

The older method, with a cane is still the best, but as it involves more work is not often seen today. A round rod is placed through the loops of the warp, and placed in a deep groove ploughed along the length of the roller. A second rod is placed on top, and when one turn is taken round the beam the warp

99 *Cane roller in cross section*

is securely held. The considerable advantage of this method is that there are no knots or cords to spoil the smooth surface of the beam. The only disadvantage is that when the last m (yd) or so of warp is reached, cords have to be fastened to the warp beam and the cane to allow the end of the warp to come over the back beam and up to the harness.

Lacing with loom cord is a simple and straightforward way of joining the back stick to the beam. It is easy to adjust, and to replace when worn out. Several holes, usually four on any loom up to 110 cm (42 in.) wide, are drilled through the beam, and doubled cords threaded through, put through their own loops, and tied on to the back stick. The drawback of this method is that the cords build up on the beam as they are wound on, and warp laths have to be put on immediately to give a true surface for winding on. A way of overcoming this is to use diagonal lacing. One end of

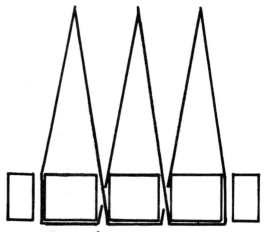

100 *Lacing a beam*

loom cord is taken down through the first hole, back up through the second, down the third, and up the fourth; then it returns in the same way down the third and up the second. A stick is now put through the two loops, the free end tied to the same stick, and the cord worked through till the stick reaches the position of the heddles. The cord is cut from the ball, and the two ends joined with a sheet bend. This knot is now worked down until it enters one of the holes. Short lengths of cord are attached to the back stick with a lark's head, and tied to the three loops with a snitch knot. The advantage of the diagonal lacing is that the cords wind in an even spiral from the holes to the knots, thereby evenly covering the warp beam. A woollen warp may be wound directly over the lacing, and if warp laths have to be used for a linen or a similarly inelastic warp, they lie evenly on the lacing. If the warp reaches beyond the last holes on the roller, two extra single cords can be run from these holes to the ends of the back stick.

The apron causes more trouble than lacing. When the cloth stretches unevenly, it cannot be straightened without removing the nails and renailing it, and making and replacing an apron which becomes too weak entails far more work than renewing the lacing. If the apron has been hemmed along the edges to prevent fraying, the hems can cause enough difference in the diameter of the beam to give trouble with the warp tension, and the apron stick and ties entail extra work in keeping them covered when beaming.

5 Knots

The following selection of knots will cover all the needs of the hand weaver. Though there are many more which are useful, they only duplicate one or other of the knots given here, with perhaps a slight saving of time or increase in efficiency.

Throughout the description of the knots, the thread or cord which starts in the right hand is referred to as the R thread or cord for the whole knot, even when it passes to the left side of the knot. The main length is called the R thread or cord, and the free end is the R end.

(1) Weavers knot or sheet bend

The end from the warp beam is always held in the left hand while the right hand ties the knot, thus preventing the thread from being pulled into the layers of warp beneath it on the beam, and so shortening it, which would result in it breaking again within the m (yd). There are two versions, both equally efficient, though the first is more easily tied with thick threads, and the second with thin.

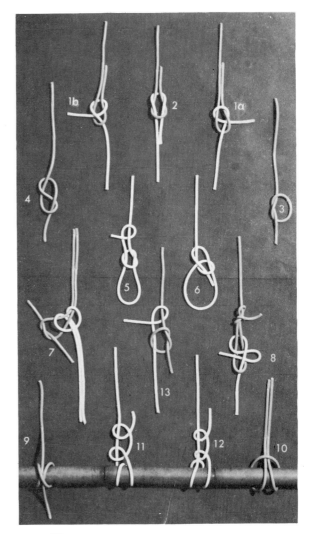

101 Knots

1 Weavers knots (a) thick thread
                  (b) thin thread
2 Reef knot
3 Thumb knot
4 Figure-of-eight knot
5 Loom harness knot
6 Bowline
7 Snitch knot
8 Single cord snitch knot
9 Clove hitch
10 Lark's head or cow hitch
11 Round turn and two half hitches
12 Modified ossel hitch
13 Span knot

a Thick thread

1 Place the R thread behind the L.
2 Take it clockwise round its own end.
3 Bring it through the middle of the knot over the L hand end.
4 Hold the R thread firmly with the last three fingers, and turn the L end over and through the knot, holding it under the L thumb.
5 Pull the R thread *only* to tighten the knot.

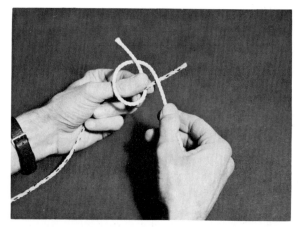

104 *Weavers knot   thick thread 3*

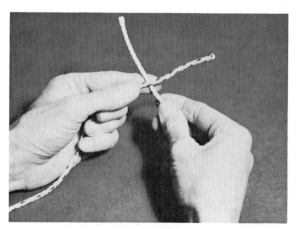

102 *Weavers knot (a) thick thread 1*

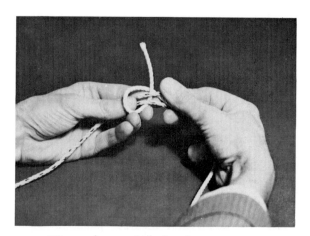

105 *Weavers knot   thick thread 4*

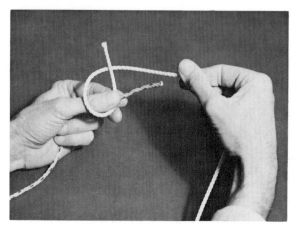

103 *Weavers knot   thick thread 2*

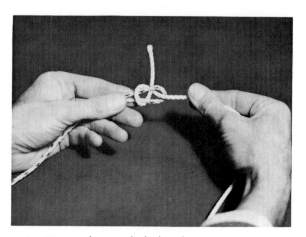

106 *Weavers knot   thick thread 5*

b Thin thread (sheet bend)

1 Place the R thread behind the L.
2 Take it clockwise round its own end.
3 Take it clockwise round the L end.
4 Hold the R thread firmly with the last three fingers, and turn the L end over and through the knot, holding it under the L thumb.
5 Pull the R thread *only* to tighten the knot.

There is a tendency for the second version particularly to capsize whilst being tied, especially if both the R end and the R thread are pulled together. When this happens all the interlacing is passed to the R thread, and L straightens and slips out of the knot.

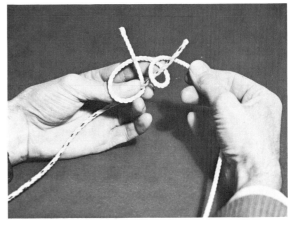

109 *Weavers knot   thin thread 3*

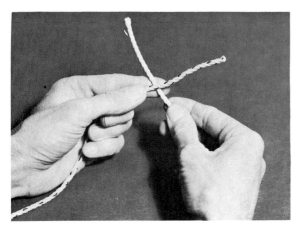

107 *Weavers knot (b) thin thread 1*

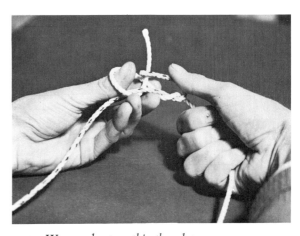

110 *Weavers knot   thin thread 4*

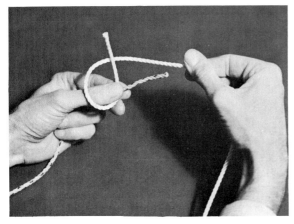

108 *Weavers knot   thin thread 2*

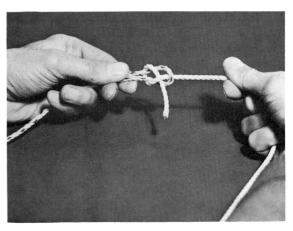

111 *Weavers knot   thin thread 5*

63

(2) Reef knot

Contrary to popular belief this is a poor knot for joining two cords. Its original use, for tying reef points on a sail, entailed its being easily undone by pulling one end over to the other cord of the knot, which capsized the knot completely, the pulled end lying straight and the other end forming two loops which slid off the now straight cord. A knot in new loom cord is very prone to do this as soon as it is used. The second version of the weavers knot is a far better knot to use.

The two halves of the reef knot follow the *same* sequence to the L and then to the R.

1. Place the R cord behind the L.
2. Bring the R end forward, down, and up behind the L cord.
3. Place the original R end behind the L.
4. Bring the R end forward, down and up behind the L cord.
5. Pull the cords to tighten (if using thick stiff cord both ends and cord may need pulling).

(3) Thumb knot

1. Take the end anti-clockwise over the cord and down behind it.
2. Bring the end up through the loop.

(4) Figure-of-eight

1. Take the end anti-clockwise over the cord and down behind it.
2. Bring the end up to the R of the cord *outside* the loop.
3. Tuck the end down through the loop.

Both the thumb knot and figure-of-eight are used to stop a cord slipping through a hole in a part of the mounting. The figure-of-eight is more efficient, as it forms a flat ring of cord against the edge of the hole.

(5) Loom harness knot

1. Tie a thumb knot well up the cord, but bring only the loop through, not the end.
2. Take the end anti-clockwise over the cord, down behind it, and up through the loop just made.

Both the loom harness knot and the bowline (below) provide loops for snitch knots. The loom harness knot is more generally useful, the height can be adjusted more easily, and the knot brings the sides of the loop together, instead of apart as the bowline.

(6) Bowline

1. Tie a thumb knot in the cord.
2. Bring the end upwards and outwards, straightening the end and putting the whole loop in the cord.
3. Take the end anti-clockwise behind the cord, and then forward and down through the loop alongside itself.

This version with the end inside the loop instead of outside is much quicker to tie, and as secure as the more usual version.

(7) Snitch knot

This is the one absolutely essential knot for adjusting a loom. It is best made with the loop coming up from below, as it is easier to hold the loop on the fingers and pull the ends through, than to do the opposite when holding the weight of a march and several treadles on the cord in the L hand. It consists of a larks head in the loop, and half a reef knot in the ends.

1. Pick up the loop on the thumb and two fingers.
2. Turn the hand over, bringing the thumb and fingers outside the two cords, and then together.
3. Slip the L half of the loop onto the fingers to join the R half, withdraw the thumb, and put it through the loop alongside the fingers to grasp the two ends coming down.
4. Pull the ends through and tighten the loop.
5. Tie the first half of a reef knot in the two ends, and tighten against the loop.

The cords making the reef must bend equally in the knot, or the knot will slip. To loosen the knot to adjust or untie, hold the two ends and push the loop upwards, then untie the half reef.

(8) Single cord snitch

This is useful when a single cord is adequate to join the two parts of the loom, but it must be adjustable. An example is the cord from the treadle to the operating lever on a dobby or witch.

1. Tie a loop (loom harness knot) in the upper cord.
2. Bring the lower end up through the loop, anti-clockwise round the back, and tuck the end between the cord and the loop.

To make it easy to undo the knot has been 'slipped', i.e. a loop instead of an end has been tucked through to complete the knot.

(9) Clove hitch

This is used for tying retaining cords to undrilled cross sticks or shaft sticks etc.; when the cord has been threaded through the hole in a drilled shaft or cross stick, the knot is tied round its own main part.

1 Bring the end down in front of the stick, and up behind it to the L.
2 Cross over to the R.
3 Repeat 1, and bring the end up and across in front of its cord again.

This knot is virtually two blanket stitches.

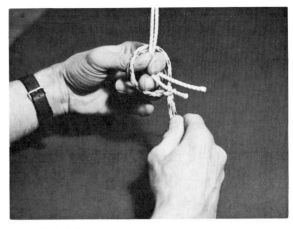

114   *Snitch knot 3*

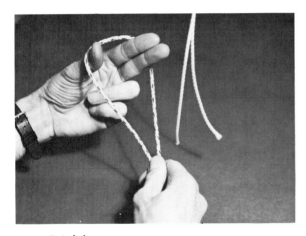

112   *Snitch knot 1*

115   *Snitch knot 4*

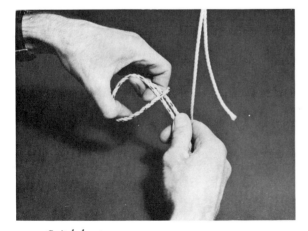

113   *Snitch knot 2*

116   *Snitch knot 5*

(10) Lark's head or cow hitch

This is another knot which is used a great deal in the mounting of the loom.

  1 Take the loop down in front of the stick, and then up behind it.

  2 Tuck the ends through the loop.

Often this knot is formed in the manner given for a snitch knot, and the knot slid on to the end of a stick, or the two ends brought over the stick, round the back and up again, and tied on top of the cords, to make what is in effect still a lark's head.

(11) Round turn and two half hitches

This is used for fastening single cords to sticks, such as in the mounting of a table loom.

  1 Make a full turn round the stick, which means tucking the end under twice.

  2 Tie a clove hitch, which is composed of two half hitches, round the cord.

If the thumb and first finger of one hand pinch the round turn firmly while the other hand ties the two half hitches, this knot can be tied accurately even with a weight on the stick. The shafts of a table loom can be adjusted for height by raising the lever, taking the round turn, pulling the cord upwards until the height is correct, and then completing the knot.

(12) Modified ossel hitch

This knot is similar in construction and use to the previous one. The second part of the turn is taken in the opposite direction round the stick, before the two half hitches are added, enabling the knot to be tied under far greater tension than the other.

(13) Span knot

This is used primarily for joining the two ends of a broken warp thread under tension. If knots are to be avoided in the warp, a m (yd) or so of warp thread is fixed round a pin in the cloth, and is threaded through the reed and heddle towards the back of the loom. The thumb knot is tied on the remaining part of the broken thread, and the half hitch put round it with the new piece set in. The thumb knot is tightened, and the tension of the warp held by pinching together the end of the thumb knot and the set-in piece of warp thread until the half hitch is tightened into place. Both knots are usually 'slipped', i.e. have a loop tucked through instead of the end to facilitate undoing the knot later (see single cord

snitch). When the span knot approaches too near to the heddles it is undone and retied further back, until finally the original end of the warp can be re-threaded and fastened round a pin in the cloth.

(14) String heddles

Though there is rarely any necessity to knot string heddles in quantity, an odd one is needed occasionally to correct an error in threading or to replace a worn one, which has broken during weaving. The method is the same as on the heddle block, the string being looped round the lower heddle stick, and the position of the knots judged by referring to the next heddle.

The knot used is a granny, solely because it will jam tightly and not capsize easily. It is tied by putting 2 half hitches with one end round the other, and cap-sizing them into place as they are tied. The end knot is a triple knot, the first two half hitches lying on the string together, and facing the same way. The third hitch is jammed against the second by pulling it onto the other cord of the knot.

  1 The left cord is brought up to the right, with the second and third fingers between them.

  2 The left second finger pulls the cord through on the back of the first joint.

  3 The hitch is pulled down into position with the left hand.

  4 The second hitch is tied in the same way, and pulled down with the *right* hand, so that the two hitches jam together.

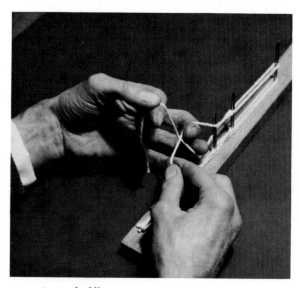

117 *String heddle 1*

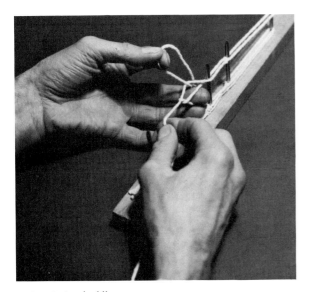

118 *String heddle 2*

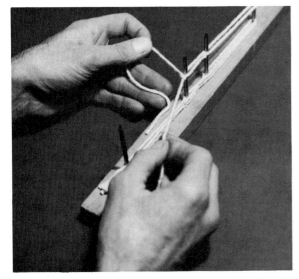

119 *String heddle 3*

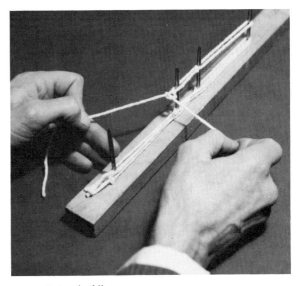

120 *String heddle 4*

(15) *The triple knot*

   1 The first two hitches facing the same way, and pulled tight with the left hand.

   2 The third hitch pulled down with the right hand.

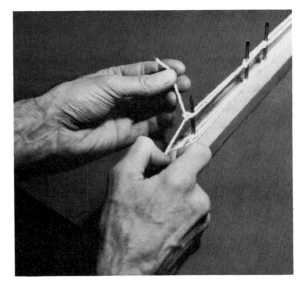

121 *String heddle 5*

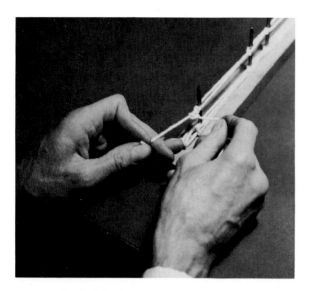

122 *String heddle 6*

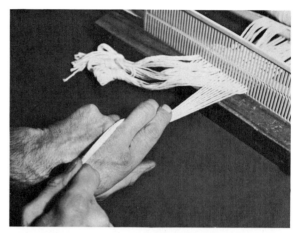

123 *Slipped thumb knot in a bunch of warp threads 1*

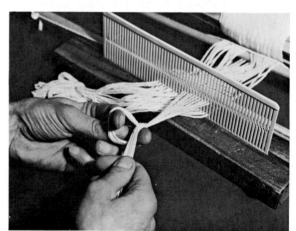

124 *Slipped thumb knot in a bunch of warp threads 2*

(16) Slipped thumb knot or overhand loop

1. Hold the bunch of threads in the right hand, and put the first two fingers of the left hand under to the right, and then over and across to the left.

2. Take the right end towards the loom, and at the same time turn the left hand completely over. The thumb is placed in the knot and the end hooked through by the second finger.

3. Pull the loop and tighten. The more this knot is pulled away from the loom, (e.g. by a reed falling forward), the tighter it becomes. It is undone by pulling the free end, but if this is difficult, take half the ends of the threads in each hand and pull apart sideways.

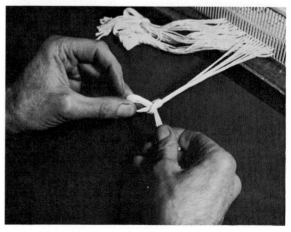

125 *Slipped thumb knot in a bunch of warp threads 3*

6 Faults

There is little to go wrong with the loom itself, as distinct from the mounting, unless the timber warps. A back, breast or knee beam must be replaced, though occasionally when two beams warp they can be placed to cancel each other out as a temporary measure. If a roller partially splits, and develops a 'shake', the diameter increases where the shake is widest, and the roller must be re-turned or replaced. The racks, on which rest the tongues supporting the batten, can usually be moved a few cm (in.) each way to correct any twist on the swords. In severe cases it may be necessary for one tongue to be placed in the next groove to bring the batten in line at warp level. The tongue should be on the front of the top tie bar, so that it is over the centre of the race block.

7 Maintenance

A regular check on all screws, bolts and wedges should be made, so that the loom does not develop any movement. Once a joint works really loose the wood can bruise round it and it will never again be tight. Pulleys, even wooden ones working on a steel spindle, will be better for oiling occasionally, though the spindles for coupers, marches and treadles need not be oiled.

Worn cords ought to be replaced before commencing a new length of weaving, and if possible, should be stretched before use to save frequent adjustment in the first m (yd) or two.

Fly shuttle looms need much more frequent oiling on the slide bar for the pick, and on the box changing mechanism. The bearings of the shuttle rollers should be adjusted and oiled when necessary, and always before commencing a new piece of work.

Dobbies and witches also need oil on the quickly or lightly moving parts, and grease (or vaseline) on the heavier parts, such as the cam and follower.

Shuttles, except for fly shuttles, require nothing more than a touch with fine glass paper if the nose becomes badly bruised. They usually pick up sufficient oil from the wool if used for tweed, to keep a smooth surface. If used exclusively for cotton or synthetic yarns, an occasional polish helps.

A warping mill needs oiling at the top and bottom bearings, and if fitted with a heck block and spreader, needs oiling lightly on the guide rollers and pulleys.

A rice needs oiling on the spindles.

A bobbin winder needs thin oil on the spindle bearings and the worm wheel spindle, and grease on the worm and worm wheel. The latter is particularly important if excessive wear is to be avoided, as there is considerable sliding movement between the worm and wheel.

All ancillary equipment, like the loom, should be checked regularly for loose screws and wedges.

Weaving

The quality of a piece of hand woven cloth depends considerably on the evenness of the tensions of the warp and weft threads. This is particularly so in the case of the weft threads, which should lie easily in the cloth, and this depends in turn on the way that the shuttle is thrown and drawn out of the shed, and on well wound bobbins or pirns.

The original shuttle bobbins were wound on goose quills or reeds and the thin brown paper tubes frequently used in hand weaving are still called quills. They are gradually giving way to the wooden bobbins which hold more yarn, and run more easily; though the latter is not entirely an advantage, as the tensioning cannot be done with a sprung spindle in a bobbin as well as was possible in the old quills, but has to be done in the throwing. On the heavy shuttles, which are to be preferred for most work, the long tapered pirns are used. They hold more yarn than bobbins, and as they wind over the end are equally free running from beginning to end. Bobbins run more freely the larger they are wound, and when nearly empty drag appreciably as they have to rotate faster. This tightens the weft, and gradually causes the warp colour to shaw up more towards the end of the bobbin.

a (i) Both *bobbins and pirns* must be wound firmly with a steady strong tension, so that the unwinding yarn as it runs off cannot cut into the lower layers and tangle or jerk as it runs. The best way to obtain smooth running is to have the yarn unwinding from the narrow to the wide end of a conical surface. In this way the yarn is never unwinding over the turn which is next to come off, and will often come off with it and jerk the yarn, if it does not actually tangle. This means traversing slowly from the wide end to the narrow when winding, and then going back sharply to the wide end for the next layer. The thread traversed quickly back up the cone cannot bring the lower layer with it when it unwinds if the tension is firm on the layer, as it crosses it at a steep angle.

To apply this in practice to a pirn, which unwinds over the end, is easy; a small cone is built up at the base, and then this conical shape is maintained all the way up the pirn. The main things to watch are firstly, maintaining the strong tension on the thread, and secondly, never going back beyond the end of the previous layer, even if this means a pirn which varies in diameter here and there. If the spindle of the bobbin winder is not large enough for the pirn, it can be built up permanently with gummed brown paper strip, or temporarily with several layers of thin warp yarn wound on tightly.

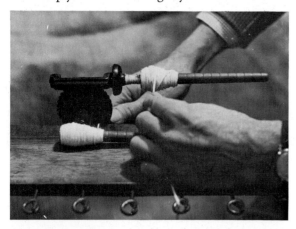

126 *Pirn winding*

A bobbin unwinds from the side, through an eye in the centre of the shuttle. Even when the eye is a long slot, the thread unwinds along the bobbin from the ends towards the centre for most of the time. This means that the two ends should be wound like miniature pirns facing each other, first one being built up and then the other, until they meet in the centre, when the last section can be filled slowly from side to side. As well as giving better unwinding from the conical surface, there are two other big advantages. The fluctuations of diameter are so rapid that they have no effect on the weft tension, and there is none of the steadily increasing tension that results

from the decreasing diameter of a bobbin wound from end to end and layer by layer. As the bobbin unwinds for some time from each end alternately, it is not continually jerked backwards and forwards along the spindle to the detriment of the tension. This is particularly important when using a paper quill, as the ends become soft and ragged from being dragged against the ends of the bobbin cavity, and again cause bad variations in tension.

127 *Bobbin winding*

Bobbins and pirns are both started by taking a single turn round the tube, crossing the thread over its own end and holding it firmly as the winding is commenced; then when the last of the yarn unwinds there is no sudden check or jerk to spoil the selvedge and the weft tension.

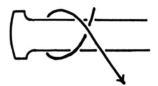

128 *Starting a bobbin or pirn*

Quills are cut from brown paper in the shape of an oval some 8 cm (3 in.) long; the width depends on the length of the bobbin cavity in the shuttle, and for smooth running must not exceed two-thirds of the length of the cavity, even when it has a long eye. This brings the width to about 5–6 cm (2–2½ in.) for most shuttles. The quill should never be made so long that it almost fills the cavity, as it is then bound to affect the tension adversely. A short quill can slide along the spindle and bring the unwinding thread more or less in line with the end of the eye, without forcing the end of the quill against the wood at the opposite end of the bobbin cavity, causing friction and increased tension.

a (ii) *Twist* When a yarn unwinds over the end of the package, each revolution round the package puts one opposite revolution into the yarn, i.e. if the yarn is unwinding clockwise round the package when looking down on it, it has the same effect as twisting the end of the yarn vertically above it anti-clockwise (Z twist). If this twist is added to the spinning twist, the yarn is hardened; if against the spinning twist, it is softened. If pirns are wound over the end from spools or cops, the twist put into the yarn by this winding can be taken out in the weaving (as the pirn unwinds) or vice versa, to leave the yarn in its original state. Both twists can be added to or subtracted from the yarn to harden or soften it. Care must be taken to ensure that the weft is softened rather than hardened, unless specifically required otherwise.

When yarns are doubled on the doubling stand, the twist of each package must be checked carefully. If doubling two dissimilar yarns of opposite spins, it is usually better to soften the thicker one and harden the thinner.

b (i) When a bobbin is put into the shuttle, a better lead is given to the thread if the bobbin unwinds from underneath.

The shuttle is held with the thumb on top, first finger on the tip, and the second and third fingers underneath, and is placed in the shed with the nose against the reed and the back slightly away from it. The throw is a flat, skimming motion of the hand, and it should begin gradually and end with a flick of the first finger as the shuttle leaves the hand. The shuttle should never be jerked, or worse still drawn back and then jerked into the shed, as this ruins the tension of the weft. As the weaver acquires speed the shuttle is obviously not placed at rest in the shed and then thrown, but swung into it with one continuous movement.

To catch the shuttle the first finger is placed on the race to lift the nose as it emerges from the warp, and the thumb is held above to trap it. The batten is held back by the last three fingers pressing against the race block. As the shuttle enters the hand it is withdrawn sideways in line with the batten. At the same time the weight of the shuttle is taken by the last

129 *Throwing the shuttle*

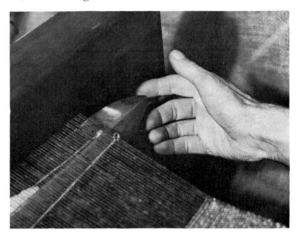

130 *Catching the shuttle*

131 *Drawing the shuttle out of the shed*

three fingers, so that the first finger can be placed on the tip of the shuttle ready for the next throw.

The natural movement would be swinging the arm back, but this pulls the weft down to the fell of the cloth at the selvedge and traps it, preventing it from taking its own tension when beaten up.

b (ii) When three or more shuttles are used they must be placed in order on the cloth, but two can be held in the hands all the time. The best way to learn this technique is to hold a spare shuttle in each hand and throw an empty shuttle, beating up between each throw.

134 *Catching with two shuttles*

The pressure on the batten is applied in a modified way while catching.

132 *Holding two shuttles while practising*

When weaving pick and pick the second shuttle to enter the hand can be caught either above or below the first, depending on which way the threads need interlocking at the selvedge.

The throwing and catching are much as before, except that the last one or two fingers hold the second shuttle whilst throwing.

133 *Throwing with two shuttles*

135 *General position at the loom ready to throw*

c Fly shuttle The fly or flying shuttle is an essential for wide warps, though it is little if anything faster than a hand thrown shuttle for warps up to 110 cm (42 in.) wide. With two or three shuttle boxes on the batten, shuttle changing is speedy and simple, but for practical purposes the number of shuttles is

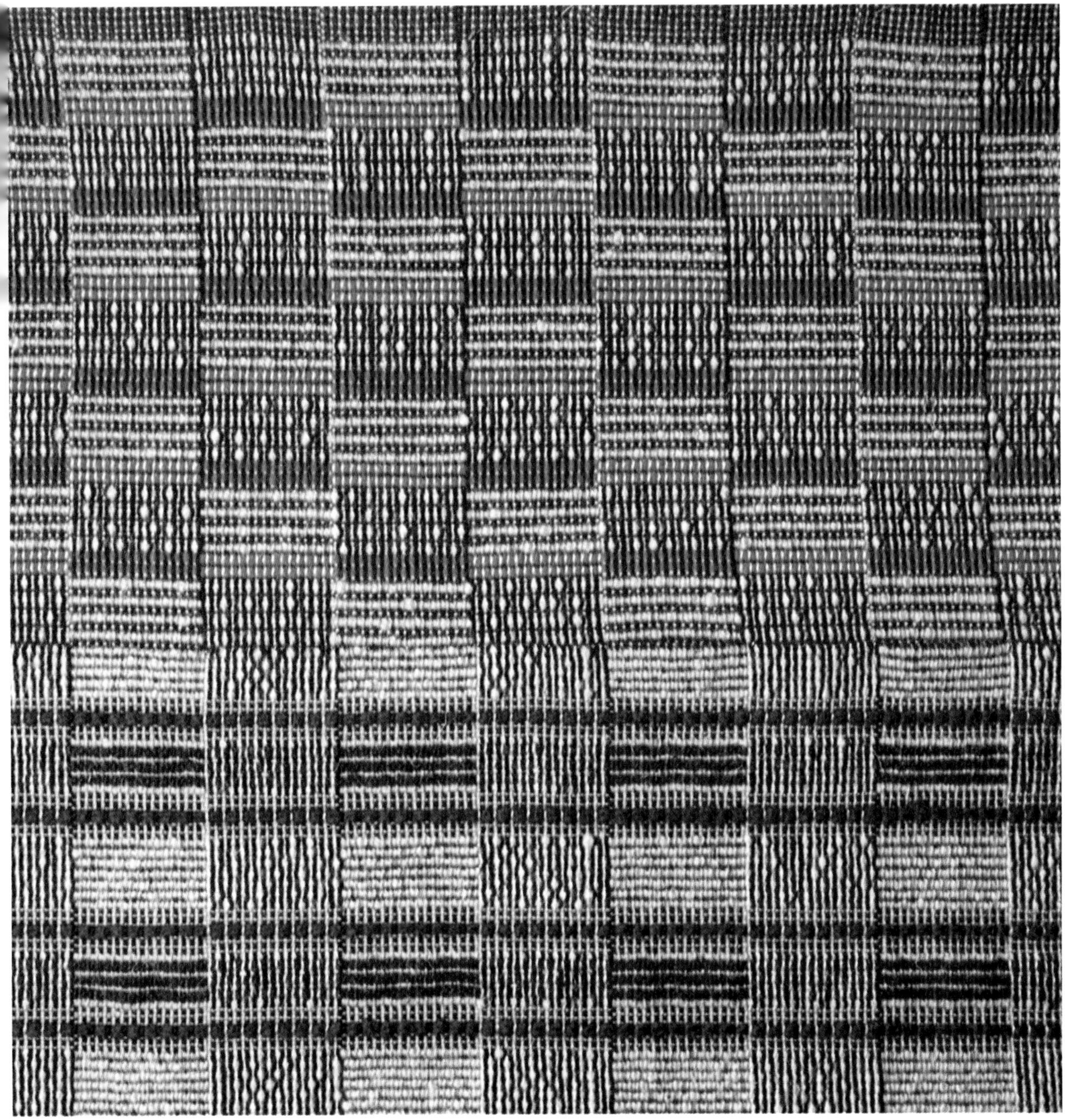

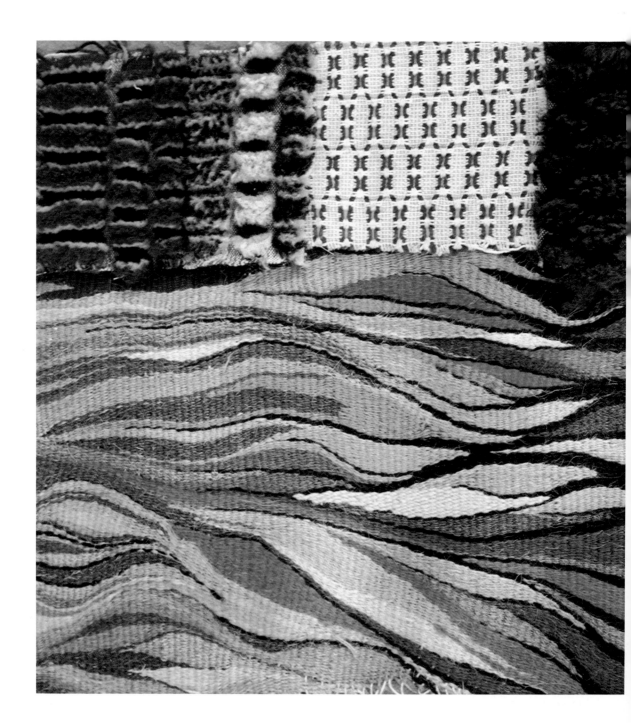

limited to the number of boxes. It is impracticable to be continually removing and replacing extra shuttles.

The shuttle is placed in either box, with the outer nose of the shuttle touching the pick of leather, or leather faced wood. The right hand holds the picking stick, or the handle on the string, and the left hand rests on the centre of the batten cap. The pick is pulled towards the weaver gently, until the weight of the shuttle is felt, and then increasingly faster till the shuttle is flicked out of the box into the shed. As soon as the shuttle is clear of the box, the pick in the other box is pulled about half way up the box to meet the shuttle. Just before the shuttle strikes the pick, the pick is released gradually so that the pick and the shuttle are going in the same direction at the moment of impact. The momentum of the shuttle is absorbed by letting the pick down to the back of the box at a steadily reducing rate. The shuttle should just be at rest as it reaches the back of the box. It is as difficult to let the shuttle down without stopping it prematurely or letting it rebound as to propel it across the shed. If the shuttle projects from the box at all, it prevents the boxes being changed. The changing device is worked by the left hand at the centre of the batten, and either slides from side to side, or has a thumb catch and a small lever. The former type moves one set of boxes up and the other down, to bring one top and the other bottom box in line together. The latter type moves both sides up or down together. De-pressing the lever raises the boxes, and pressing the thumb catch releases them so that they fall by their own weight. The sliding type is light to operate, but limited to three boxes at the most. The second type will take four, and is quicker and more positive in its action.

Changing the boxes can only be done when all the shuttles are correctly in the boxes, and both picks are at the back of the boxes on the rests. The right hand has to be in such a position that the cords to the picks are slack to allow the springs to pull back the picks.

As fly shuttle weft tension tends to be firmer than a hand thrown shuttle, beating on a closed shed is used more frequently than on an open shed, and the tenterhook is more often used.

d Weft joins The first pick of weft with a new bobbin or a new colour need not be turned in on a length of cloth as it would be on a small article like a scarf (see page 110). Five or 6 cm (2 in.) or so can be left hanging out of the selvedge, and this is trimmed off later. If two or more shuttles are in use with frequent changes of colour, the weft threads are carried up the side, and not continually cut off and re-started. When a bobbin runs out the new thread can be over-lapped 15 mm ($\frac{1}{2}$ in.) with the old one anywhere in the cloth, if the ends of yarn have been broken, as they will then taper off and the join will not show. If, in a coarse fabric, such a join is obtrusive, the old yarn is turned in on the next shed for about 20 mm ($\frac{3}{4}$ in.), and the new one left hanging as before.

1 Sequence of operation

The height of the bench or stool is of more im-portance than is generally recognised, and a com-fortable position will make for quicker, more accurate, and less tiring weaving. The treadles should reach the fully open position (touching the floor) without having to stretch the legs too far, and the elbows should be just clear of the breast beam when the arms are at the sides. If it proves to be impossible to satisfy both these requirements, set the stool high enough for the elbows to clear the beam, and fix a length of wood under the loom to act as a stop for the treadles.

The sequence of the operations depends on the type of cloth, most cloths need beating on the open shed, but weft faced cloths, and especially rugs, need beating on the closed shed.

Until the shed is closed, the weft is free to move along the *width* of the cloth. If the beat is made with the shed open the weft is taken into the shed slightly as the reed comes forward and stretches the cloth to its full width. The shed is changed whilst the reed is against the fell of the cloth, helping to give a good 'cover' (see page 50), and on the backward stroke the reed clears the shed for the next pick. The beating and changing of the shed may usually proceed simultaneously, as long as the shed is only just closed at the moment of impact, and not beginning to open the other way. The weight of the body can be swung forward on to the treadles to open the shed, and backwards when beating up, and the feet are moving to the next treadles.

A weft faced cloth needs a slack weft to distort round the warp threads, which lie straight in the cloth and conceal them. The weft is thrown in, and the shed is changed. This traps the weft, and when the beat follows the slack is distributed across the cloth.

The length of the beat must be watched, and free use must be made of the rack on the top of a foot power loom for adjusting the position of the beater. It is better to weave little more than the length of this rack and wind on more frequently, than to try and weave as much as possible between each winding on. A series of even graduations of colour from that of one yarn predominating to that of the other is frequently due to the difference in the length of the beat.

When recommencing work after an appreciable interval, it is as well to beat up lightly once with the shed open, and once with it closed before throwing a new pick, as the picks tend to creep back away from the fell. This slight creeping back also means that the last two or three picks never look as heavily beaten as the rest of the cloth, but by the time they are fifteen or twenty picks down from the fell, they will be as close as the rest.

2 Treadling sequence

The quickest way of working over the treadles is to use the two feet alternately, and use the toe and heel alternately on each foot. As the foot is never jumped from one treadle to another, there is never any confusion as to which treadle is being used, and one foot can be commencing the downward movement while the other is coming up, as long as both feet do not press on the treadles at the same time and strain the cords of the mounting.

a The easiest order of treadling starts at the sides and works in to the centre. On the four shaft twill or similar weaves this would give the order 1–3–4–2; with the left toe on 1, left heel on 3, and the right toe and heel on 2 and 4 respectively. If the foot not being used rests lightly on its treadles, the feet need not be moved away. As one foot depresses a treadle, the other foot is simultaneously moved to the treadle needed for the following shed. When working on eight treadles a similar plan is followed, 1–3–5–7–8–6–4–2, with a similar toe and heel sequence used both inwards and outwards.

b If the number of treadles being used gives an uncomfortably wide stretch, the treadling can be done from left to right with both feet, starting from the centre for the right foot, 1–3–5–7–2–4–6–8. This is equally as quick to do, but care must be taken to keep the beat level, as the body tends to tilt from side to side.

c Certain types of weave require modification of this plan. A flush spot (or Bronson) weave requires every second row on the plain treadle, so this is placed at one side of the loom, preferably the side away from the pivot of the marches, to make it light to work, and the other treadles are all worked over by the other foot.

The traditional overshot weave needs the two plain weave treadles alternately with one of the pattern treadles, and this can follow a similar plan; the two plain treadles to one side, and four pattern treadles to the other, with one foot for the ground, and the other for the pattern.

A gauze or a leno weave needs the open and crossed sheds on one foot, and the standard shed on the other. When weaving plain, either the open or the crossed, the feet are used alternately, and when weaving pure gauze, although the same foot is used for both open and crossed sheds, there is less strain on the harness and warp if the standard shed is always treadled between the open or crossed sheds to clear the doups.

When an irregular treadling plan is used it is often better to tie the same shed to two different treadles on different sides of the loom to save jumping back with one foot, and though it increases the number of treadles, the consequent gain in the regularity of treadling makes it worth doing.

d Double foot ties Certain weaves require two ground treadles to be combined with a number of other treadles at different times and in different combinations. While for small harnesses it is quite feasible to tie a fresh treadle for each combination, larger harnesses of say eight shafts upwards could easily require more treadles than there are on the loom. The double foot tie-up overcomes this problem, by giving two ground treadles to one foot, and the other treadles to the other foot, one of each set being used simultaneously. Often one ground treadle is held for several rows, the other foot working over the other set, or the ground may change every pick, whilst the other set changes every second pick. This would otherwise entail a large number of treadles or much jumping with both feet. One special use of the double foot tie is for tying up a counter march loom for experimental work. There are fourteen possible sheds with four shafts, but the double foot tie reduces the number of treadles from fourteen to eight (see page 80).

3   Faults

Broken threads usually occur in or near the heddles, where the strain is greatest. Find the end that is down, either from the gap in the reed or from the porrey cross, and tie on a short length of warp using a weavers knot. Re-enter the end if necessary, put a pin into the cloth in line with the broken end, and wind the new end in a figure-of-eight two or three times round the pin. Push the point of the pin down into the cloth, and weave on for about 15 cm (6 in.), then remove it. *Never* wind the pin onto the cloth beam. If the knot is too bulky to weave over or would spoil the fabric use a span knot instead (see page 66 and fig. 101).

Slack or tight ends are cut at the fell of the cloth, have a short length of warp tied on, and are then wound round a pin. When the warp and weft are of two distinct colours, a slack thread of either will show more of its own colour, and a tight one will show a line of the other colour. A regular streakiness occurring every 5–10 cm (2–4 in.), changing gradually from weft colour to warp colour, with a sharp division between the repeats, is usually caused by a heavier beat after winding on, when the batten has a greater distance to travel. It can also be caused by a bobbin or paper quill being wound in layers instead of being built up at the ends, the slacker tension with the full bobbin showing more weft colour.

If a gap between two rows of weft suddenly appears at one selvedge, tapering off to nothing by the time it reaches the other, the batten pivot tongue has jumped forward into the next groove on the rack on one side of the loom.

If a mistake has been made, it is usually better to cut out the weft, especially with woollen yarns, rather than back weave for more than two or three rows. By the time that a tweed warp has been woven and back woven it is usually so fluffy that the re-weaving is difficult, and the cloth has a different appearance from the rest. When cutting out weft, make several short cuts up between two warp threads, one just inside each selvedge, and the rest about 30 cm (1 ft) apart. Pull the cut sections of weft towards the reed, and the selvedge sections outwards by the loop.

A mistake in the weave occurring at regular intervals is due to a breakage of one of the cords of

the mounting, and may go unnoticed for several cm (in.) in certain types of cloth. A broken cord from treadles to marches or counter marches will show a mistake less frequently than one from counter marches to shafts. A knot pulled through a hole is less easy to detect, as there are no loose ends visible. The best way to locate and correct any fault in the mounting is to pull each shaft forward in turn, and look down between it and the next to check that no heddles are caught on the adjacent heddle sticks, and that there are no broken string heddles or warp ends tangled in the warp. Then tie the top heddle sticks together; on a counter march loom peg the coupers, and check all through the cording, working upwards first and then down.

If a shed steadily becomes worse, it is usually a knot pulling through the treadle or march, though it can be a knot in the upper mounting giving way. If there is no obvious fault in the mounting, but the sheds are poor, check all the cords in the mounting, making sure that all corresponding cords on both sides of the loom are equal, and that the warp line is correct.

Very occasionally the spindle of the treadles, the marches or the coupers becomes unbolted, or the split pin drops out, and the spindle creeps slowly out of the bearing at one end. This has no great effect immediately as the spindle is still held by the second bearing, and the levers at the sound end work normally while those at the loose end still work for the time being but give a smaller movement. A loose treadle spindle gives a mixture of good and bad sheds; a march or counter march spindle gives all poor sheds, with either the front or the back shafts working normally, and the couper spindle gives sheds poor at one side only, and even on the poor side the back or front shafts will work as usual. If the selvedges run tight during the weaving, a temporary cure is to put a warp lath over the tight selvedge threads on one side of the loom, under the whole of the rest of the warp, and over the tight selvedge threads on the other side, at the back of the loom just above the warp beam. Then pull the stick down and partially round the beam with the warp tension released slightly, thus tightening the threads under which the stick has been placed. The best guide to even tension is a straight weft thread. When the warp is slack, the weft springs back into the shed after beating up, whereas when the warp is tight the weft is held. When the stick is put in, the weft should be straight and if it is not, the stick or sticks must be adjusted so that it is. Often the stick can be dispensed with when nearing the end of the warp, and there is less difference between the centre and selvedge tension. More than one stick may be used; if the warp tension alters gradually from the centre to the edges, the second stick will probably need to pass under fewer threads than the first.

Slack selvedges are dealt with in a similar way, but here the sticks would of course go under the selvedge and over the body of the warp. They are often caused by an over-tight weft pulling them in, with consequent stretching each time the beat is made. Check that the bobbin or pirn is in order, and then make sure that the catching and holding of the shuttle is not at fault.

Theory

1 Calculations

a The count of yarns The count of a yarn is its size expressed as a relationship between its length and its weight (i.e. its linear density). For a given weight a finer yarn will have a greater length and for a given length a finer yarn will weight less. This is the basis of the two systems of determining counts, the fixed length or direct system and the fixed weight or indirect system. The count number in the direct system is the number of weight units that the standard length weighs, so the finer the yarn the less it weighs and the lower the count number. The opposite is true in the indirect system, as the count is the number of hanks which together weight the standard weight, so the finer the yarn the greater the number of hanks and the higher the count number.

The most important direct systems are the traditional denier system and the comparatively new tex system, which is discussed below. The denier is the now obsolete weight of one-twentieth of a gramme, the weight of the old Roman silver coin, the denarius, and the denier count is the weight in deniers of 450 metres, the standard skein for thrown silk. The denier system was used for all filament yarns, both natural silk and all the man-made fibres. The standard was the weight in grammes of 9000 metres.

The indirect systems are many and varied, and were usually based on the size of the reel on which the thread was skeined in any particular district. The circumference of the reel gave the length of the thread, and the number of turns that could be laid on without building up too much gave the size of the smallest whole skein. The threads of this first 'lay' or 'lea' (linen) would be 'cut' (Galashiels woollen) and taken off when the wooden tongue of the counting device made its 'snap' (West of England), and another 'skein' (Yorkshire woollen) made. The obvious method of comparing yarns of different thicknesses was to state how many length units together weighed one pound (British fixed weight), or some other unit of weight such as the 24 ounces of the Galashiels count. The length and weight units for any count were such that the sizes of yarns in general use in the district gave count numbers that were easy to use in calculations, but as industrial units became larger the smaller district counts became obsolete, and by the time that the tex system came into general use in Great Britain, only the worsted, the Galashiels and, to a lesser extent, the Yorkshire skein systems were in general use in the woollen and worsted industries, and the cotton count in the cotton trade.

The count number of a single yarn is given as a single figure, but when a yarn is plied, (also termed folded or doubled), both the size of the yarn and the number of plies are indicated. For all yarns except spun silk the count of the component yarns is given; in spun silk the count of the final yarn is given.

When a hank of yarn is doubled in thickness, its length will be halved; if its thickness is increased three fold, its length will be reduced to one third of the original, and so on. If, therefore, a yarn which has four hanks to the pound is doubled, instead of $4 \times \frac{1}{4}$ lb hanks, there will be $2 \times \frac{1}{2}$ lb hanks of twice the original thickness. The final plied yarn is the equivalent of a 2s singles in thickness, as in each case there are two hanks to the pound.

The count is written 2/4s, signifying two plies of 4s count. In the same way, 3/12s indicates that the yarn is of three plies of 12s count, and is equivalent to a 4s, the count of the ply always being divided by the number of plies to obtain the final count.

The tex system is a direct decimal system based on the SI metric units and is recommended by the ISO for general use internationally for all fibres. The units are the gramme and the kilometre and the count number is the weight in grammes of one kilometre. The multiple kilotex, the weight in kilogrammes of one kilometre is recommended for slivers and thick soft yarns and the sub-multiple millitex (mg/km) for continuous filament yarns. In the tex system the count of plied yarns can be

stated in two ways, either by the prefix 'R' (for resultant count) followed by the count of the final yarn and then the ply, e.g. R 60 tex/2, or by giving the count of the component yarns and then the number of plies, e.g. 30 tex × 2. Both examples indicate a two–ply yarn of 60s final count.

The table below gives the standards for some of the most common yarn count systems and the conversion factors to tex.

Table of yarn count conversion factors

Direct systems	Unit of weight	Unit of length	Conversion factor
Tex	gramme	km	1
Denier	gramme	9 km	0.1111

To convert:
  Denier to tex, multiply denier by the conversion factor
  Den × CF = Tex
  Tex to denier, divide tex by the conversion factor
  $\dfrac{\text{Tex}}{\text{CF}} = \text{Den}$

Indirect systems	Unit of length	Unit of weight	Conversion factor
Cotton	840 yd hank	1 lb	590.5
Silk, spun	840 yd hank	1 lb	590.5
Woollen			
Galashiels	300 yd cut	24 oz	2 480 (= 200 yd/lb)
Yorkshire skein	256 yd skein	1 lb	1938
Worsted	560 yd hank	1 lb	885.8
Linen (wet spun)	300 yd lea	1 lb	1 654
American cut	300 yd cut	1 lb	1 654
American run	100 yd run	1 oz	310
Metric	1 kilometre	1 kg	1 000

To convert:
  Any indirect count to tex, divide the conversion factor by the count
  $\dfrac{\text{CF}}{\text{count}} = \text{Tex}$
  Tex to any indirect count, divide the conversion factor by the tex count
  $\dfrac{\text{CF}}{\text{Tex}} = \text{Count}$

Tex is used for all yarns.

Denier is used for all continuous filament yarns, both natural (thrown silk), and man-made.

b Cloth calculations The only calculation frequently made by hand weavers is to find the approximate weight of yarn required for a particular length of cloth, the type of yarns and the sett being already decided upon. Occasionally there is the need to find the sett of an unknown yarn. Comparison with known yarns is possible, but inaccurate, as a difference in twist can cause considerable apparent difference in the size of yarns of a similar count. Winding the warp thread round a stick (just touching) gives a rough guide, the number of threads which go into a centimetre (inch) giving the 'diameter number' of the thread. It is more accurate to calculate the diameter of the thread, and then in either case calculate the sett from the diameter number.

1 *To find the weight of warp required:*

| Width of cloth in cm (inches) | × | no. of threads per cm (inch) | = | Total no. of threads. |

W (width) × S (sett) = Threads. Total

| Length of one warp thread in metres (yd) | × threads | = Total length of warp. |

Therefore:

$$\text{Length(L)} \times \text{width(W)} \times \text{sett(S)} = \frac{\text{Total length of warp}}{\text{(m or yd)}}$$
(m or yd) (cm or in.)

$$\frac{\text{Length in metres}}{1\,000} \times \text{tex} = \text{weight in grammes.}$$

and

$$\frac{\text{Length in yards}}{\text{Yards per pound}} = \text{weight in pounds}$$

Therefore:

$$\frac{L(m) \times W(cm) \times S \times \text{tex}}{1\,000} = \text{weight (grammes)}$$

and

$$\frac{L\,(yd) \times W\,(in.) \times S}{C\,(count) \times St\,(standard)} = \text{weight (pounds)}$$

('Standard' is the length of the standard hank or skein in the count system of the yarn being used.)

e.g.

L = 5m, W = 80 cm, S = 6 ends/cm, tex = 300.

$$\frac{5 \times 80 \times 6 \times 300}{1\,000} = \frac{2\,400 \times 300}{1\,000} = 720 \text{ grammes.}$$

In a square cloth the weight of weft will be the same as the weight of warp. If not square, substitute the number of picks per centimetre (inch) for the sett, as the number of centimetres (inches) of weft to weave one centimetre (inch) of cloth is the same proportion as the number of metres (yards) to weave one metre (yard) of cloth.

2 *To find the length of a warp:*
Finished length of the cloth + 10% take-up and shrinkage + loom wastage of 0.5 to 0.75 metres (20-26 in.) for table or foot-power looms respectively.

e.g.

Finished length	5.00
10% take-up and shrinkage	0.50
waste, foot-power loom	0.75
	6.25 metres

3 *The count of plied yarns:*
If the count is given in the form R (count) tex/(ply): The final or 'resultant' count is given.
If the count is given in the form (count)tex × (ply): The final count is given by count × ply.
e.g.
Two 30 tex yarns plied together to make a 60 tex yarn can be stated as either:

R 60 tex/2
or 30 tex × 2   (30 × 2 = 60)

In imperial units, the count of a plied yarn is given as a fraction; usually, though not always, the number of plies precedes the count of the component yarn. A yarn of three plies of 12s count would therefore be stated as being a 3/12s yarn. The count of the plied yarn by the number of plies, e.g. a 3/12s yarn is $\frac{12}{3} = 4$s final count.

4 *To find the length per unit of weight:*
Tex count = Weight of 1km in grammes.

Therefore:

$\dfrac{1 \text{ (km)}}{\text{tex}} =$ km per gramme and $\dfrac{1000}{\text{tex}} =$ km per kilogramme.

Imperial count = number of standard hanks per pound.

Therfore:

count × standard = yards per pound.

5　*To find the diameter of a yarn:*
There is no method of calculating the diameter of a tex-count yarn without having recourse to tables of specific density or volume of the raw materials, so the table below gives the diameter and diameter number of yarns from 50 to 300 tex (2/20s to 2/4s cotton, 50 cut to 8 cut Galashiels, 38 to 6 skein Yorkshire woollen and 17s to 3s worsted).

Table 1

Tex count	*Diameter in mm*			*Diameter number*		
50	*0.26*	**0.28**	*0.32*	*38*	**36**	*31*
75	*0.32*	**0.34**	*0.39*	*31*	**29**	*26*
100	*0.37*	**0.39**	*0.42*	*27*	**26**	*24*
150	*0.45*	**0.48**	*0.52*	*22*	**21**	*19*
200	*0.52*	**0.55**	*0.60*	*19*	**18**	*17*
250	*0.58*	**0.62**	*0.67*	*17*	**16**	*15*
300	*0.63*	**0.68**	*0.73*	*16*	**15**	*14*

The centre column of each set (in heavy type) gives the average values suitable for most fibres. The first and third columns (in italics) give the values for viscose rayon and nylon respectively

Yarns of 200 tex will set at about 6 ends/cm in plain weave (approx 16 ends/in.)

The diameter number of an imperial count yarn is related to the square root of the number of yards to the pound of the yarn. For firm yarns, such as worsted and cotton, the diameter number is one-tenth less than the square root of the yards per pound, and for soft yarns, such as woollen yarns and tweed yarns, it is one-sixth less.
For firm yarns:
diameter number = $0.9 \times \sqrt{\text{count} \times \text{standard}}$
For soft yarns:
diameter number = $0.84 \times \sqrt{\text{count} \times \text{standard}}$

6　*To find the maximum sett of a yarn:*
The simplest formula is Ashenhurst's formula. The space taken up in the cloth in terms of thread widths by one repeat of the weave is equal to the number of ends of warp plus the number of times that the weft passes from one side of the fabric to the other. (See 77.) This width multiplied by the thread diameter number will give the actual width in the cloth.

Therefore:

diameter number of the yarn
$$\times \frac{\text{(ends per repeat)}}{\text{(ends + intersections)}}$$

gives the maximum sett of the yarn.

$$D \times \frac{\text{(e)}}{\text{(e + i)}} = \text{maximum sett}$$

Few cloths are woven to this standard of firmness, which gives the maximum sett possible for a 'square' cloth, i.e. with the same number of ends and picks per inch, and the same yarn for warp and weft. A good working sett is about three-quarters of this number or slightly more.

2　Weaves

This section deals with the majority of weaves and techniques likely to be of interest to the handweaver. Sufficient information is given about each weave to show the principle behind it and the type of cloth that it produces, but designing with the weave is not discussed. Once the construction of a weave is understood variations of it can easily be drafted and woven. An understanding of cloth construction gives the handweaver an unlimited opportunity for experimental work. A creative weaver will design the cloth from the very beginning, and although the traditional patterns are often used, much more satisfaction is derived from producing a length of cloth that is completely original.

The weave is the order in which the warp and weft are interlaced. For a simple two shaft loom, describing the weave presents no problem. The odd numbered ends are drawn on one shaft, and the even on the other, and the shafts are lifted alternately.

(This corresponds to the eyes and dents in the rigid heddle.)

More complicated weaves cannot be described in this way, and it is essential to understand the connection between the weave plan of any piece of cloth and the threading and lifting to produce it. For

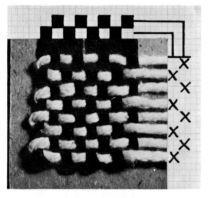

136 *Cloth with threading and lifting*

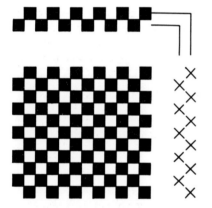

137 *Two shaft plain weave*

138 *Four shaft plain weave*

this purpose weave plans, threading drafts, and lifting plans or tie-up and treadling drafts are used. The piece of woven cloth shown in *136* is represented by the weave plan, in *137*. The black warp ends are shown running upwards through the two shafts, and the threading on alternate shafts is indicated by squares representing the heddles through which the ends are entered. The white weft is extended to the right, and crosses the two rows representing a continuation of the shafts, and on each pick the shaft raised for it is marked.

The same weave plan as 137, but threading on four shafts saves crowding the heddles on the shafts. The threading is a straight draft, shafts 1 and 3 working together and replacing shaft 1 in the two shaft draft, and controlling all the odd threads, shafts 2 and 4 likewise replacing shaft 2. The lifting plan now has to cover four shafts, and this is written as a treadling plan for a foot power loom on the far right. The draft of the tie-up between the treadles and marches is given above it, the crosses horizontally in line with the shafts indicating that they are tied to the treadle which is vertically below it. The shed for the first pick is formed by raising shafts 1 and 3 on a table loom, while on a foot power loom the treadle tied to shafts 2 and 4 must be used as this treadle will take the shafts down while raising shafts 1 and 3. Thus any lifting plan can be followed on a foot power loom, but unless the shafts required to *sink* are tied to the treadles as above, the reverse face of the cloth will be uppermost. In many weaves both faces are similar, but as most amateur weavers prefer to see the face of the cloth as they work, this point must be watched. In industry cloth is frequently woven face downwards, so that knots, joins etc. are automatically brought to the back of the cloth as it is woven, with a considerable saving of time and trouble.

In the drafts and weave plans which follow the lifting plan and tie-up and treadling will be given for the common weaves only. The lifting plan will be

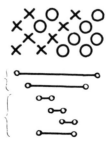

139 *Double foot tie up*

omitted in the rest of the section as it is easier to lift from a treadling plan and tie-up than vice versa.

The tie-up draft for a counter march mounting is the same as for a counter balanced; the marks are tied to the counter marches to sink as before, and the blanks are tied to the marches to rise.

The double foot tie referred to on page 74 is given below. As half of the knots of the full tie will not be used, the sinking ties are marked by a X, and the rising ties by O. The blanks are not tied.

1 PLAIN WEAVE

The simplest, plain or tabby weave, when woven with a black warp and white weft of equal thickness and equally spaced produces a plain 'square' cloth. Variations of this can be made by using threads of widely differing thicknesses; thin warp, thick weft, thick warp and thin weft, alternate thick and thin threads in both warp and weft, and by spacing some of the ends more widely than the others, or grouping some ends together and leaving a section empty. In all these examples the weave is the same, although the effect is different. These weaves are the basis of the simple texture weaving which can be done on any plain weave loom, rigid heddle or two shaft, and makes a very good introduction to the craft.

The cloth may be 'square', and light or heavy, or it may be unbalanced. An open warp allows the weft to be beaten down to cover it, the warp lying straight and the weft doing all the bending. A light fabric of this type is a weft cord (or rib), a heavy one a tapestry and a very heavy one a rug. A fine but closely set warp used with a thick weft gives the reverse effect, the weft lying straight and the warp doing all the distortion. This gives a rib running weft way, but with a warp face, and is called a warp rib. By alternating thick and thin threads in the warp

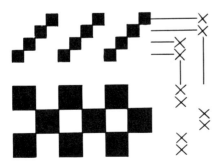

140 $\frac{2}{2}$ *hopsack*

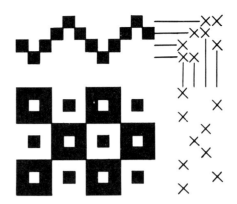

141 $\frac{3}{3}$ *stitched hopsack*

and in the weft, both cords and ribs can be given greater prominence.

2 PLAIN WEAVE DERIVATIVES—*Hopsack*

a This is a plain weave with two or more threads working together for each end and pick.

b The centre float is stitched to give firmer cloth, with a pleasant all-over pattern.

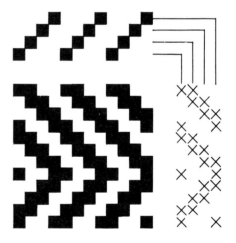

A weft faced twill is $\frac{1}{3}$.

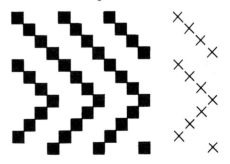

A warp faced twill is $\frac{3}{1}$.

142 *Twills,* $\frac{2}{2}$ $\frac{1}{3}$ $\frac{3}{1}$

3   TWILLS

A plain twill is a diagonal weave, in which the threads float over two or more threads of the opposite set, and the float moves one thread sideways on each successive pick. It can be woven on any number of shafts from three upwards. Balanced four shaft twill (two ends up and two down), is written $\frac{2}{2}$.

a Types of twill. Four shaft.

   (*i*)   Straight.

   (*ii*) Waved or point twill giving horizontal waved lines.

(*i*)   (*ii*)   (*iii*)   (*iv*)

143 *Types of twill*

82

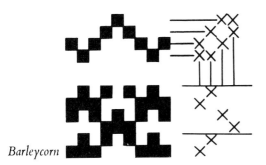

144 *Barleycorn*

(*iii*) Herringbone twill gives vertical lines of right-hand and left-hand twill, and is firmer than (*ii*).

(*iv*) Broken twill and (*v*) barley corn. Both give all-over effects for tweeds.

b Types of twill. Eight shaft

A four shaft twill has only two parts which are; equal $\frac{2}{2}$; and broad and fine, $\frac{3}{1}$ or $\frac{1}{3}$. An eight

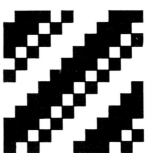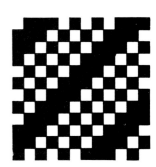

145 *Eight shaft twills*

shaft has four or six parts, and of varying thicknesses e.g. $\frac{3}{2}\frac{1}{2}$. $\frac{3}{3}\frac{1}{1}$, $\frac{3}{1}\frac{1}{1}\frac{1}{1}$ giving lines of different thicknesses. The same range of variations as in the four shaft twill is possible, e.g. straight, point etc.

4 MODIFIED TWILLS

a High angle (warp face)

(*i*) Gabardine. This is a $\frac{2}{2}$ twill, on a fine warp, but by having many more ends than picks to the cm (in.) the twill is much steeper.

(*ii*) Whipcord is produced by taking alternate ends of a twill weave, thus reducing its width.

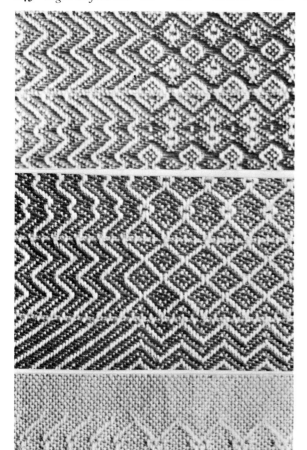

146 *Eight shaft twills*

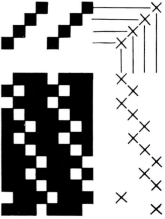

147 *Four end whipcord*

(*iii*) Mixture of weaves. The example given is a $\frac{2}{2}$ twill on the even picks and a plain weave on the odd picks, giving a firm, light cloth.

148 *High angle twill from mixed weave*

b Low angle (weft face)

This is not generally as useful as the high angle, but can be produced by:

(*i*) throwing alternate picks of a twill
(*ii*) having two weaves mixed end and end. This makes good grounds for upholstery fabrics.

5 SATIN WEAVE

a A warp faced cloth, woven with a re-arranged twill weave so that the fine diagonal of the twill is broken, and no longer stands out on the cloth. The intersection of warp and weft moves at least two ends on each pick, and is usually woven face down to save continually lifting all but one of the shafts and stressing the warp unnecessarily.

b Five shaft
c Eight shaft

149 *Five end satin*

150 *Eight end satin*

6 PLAIN WEAVE BASE

(*1*) (*a*) *Flush spot. (Bronson)*

(*i*) All-over pattern on a plain weave ground.

151 *Flush spot (Bronson) weave, spots detached*

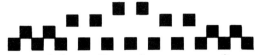

152 *Flush spots (Bronson) weave, spots adjacent*

(*ii*) Detached figures on a plain weave ground.

153 *Flush spot (Bronson) weave, detached figures on ground*

This weave has alternate ends on the front shaft, the remainder being (*i*) divided equally in small groups of two or three ends on the rest of the shafts, or (*ii*) set mainly on shaft two for the ground, with those still remaining on the rest of the shafts. Alternate sheds are plain weave (shaft 1 lifted) and pattern, for which most of the back shafts are raised, the spots being produced by flushes or floats of weft. This is often more effective with two wefts.

(*1*) (*b*) *Overshot weave* See colour plate facing page 49.

The plain ground is woven in a finer yarn, and the pattern, in a softer slightly thicker yarn, is shot over or under the ground, which is lifted in blocks.

(*i*) Standard four block. The pattern blocks blend into the ground through a half tone area on all four sides. (*154 opposite*).

(*ii*) On opposites, two block. There is no blending of colour, which changes abruptly from pattern to ground.

155 *Two block overshot weave (on opposites)*

154 *Four block overshot weave*

155a *Two-block overshot on opposites*
(Snail's Trail)

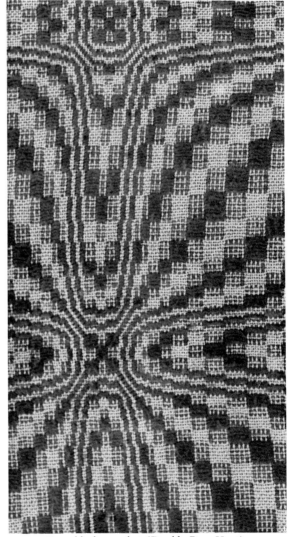

154a *Four-block overshot (Double Bow Knot)*

(2) *Sections of plain weave on pairs of shafts*

Each section of warp is threaded alternately on two shafts, and can shed independently of the sections on the other pairs of shafts.

(i) Traditional honeycomb. While one block is being woven the other is lifted to allow the weft to pass behind it, and the thick weft plain weave joins the blocks. This is better woven face down, and variations can be woven on six and eight shafts.

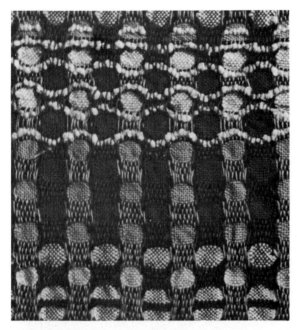

156   *Traditional honeycomb with variations*

(ii) Bedford cord. One weft weaves with the odd numbered sections and passes behind the even sections, and the second weft weaves the even sections. The floats on the back allow the front to go up in ridges when the fabric is washed.

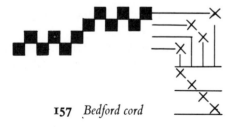

157   *Bedford cord*

(3) *Extra shafts*

In this group one set of shafts carries the cloth, and the extra shafts, behind the others, have an extra warp which works independently of the cloth, and is solely for effect, and not part of the structure of the cloth.

(i) Plain weave on two shafts

a Extra warp spot or stripe. While the ground is woven on shafts 1 and 2, 3 and/or 4 stay up or down, so that the extra warp floats above or below the cloth, interlacing only when it changes over at the end of the float.

158   *Extra warp*

b Distorted weft. Extra ends on shafts 3 and 4 about 20 mm ($\frac{3}{4}$ in.) apart; shaft 3 is floated over the ground for 15 mm ($\frac{1}{2}$ in.), 3 and 4 raised and a thick weft thrown between them and the cloth, shaft 4 floated for 15 mm ($\frac{1}{2}$ in.), then 3 and 4 raised for the thick weft again. When washed the thick weft distorts between the warp floats.

159   *Distorted weft (on extra warp threading)*

160   *Distorted weft*

(ii) Plain weave in blocks. Four shafts or more

a Coarse weave over plain weave ground. Two sets of extra warp float under and over, working in opposition, while the ground is woven plain. When the odd or even blocks of warp are raised for a pick of weft in a yarn similar to the extra warp, an effect like that given by the extra warp is produced weft way. When these two weaves are combined the extra warp and weft together make a coarse weave on top of the ground.

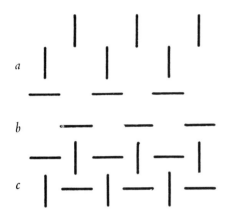

161 *Coarse weave over plain weave ground* (a) *extra warp,* (b) *extra weft,* (c) *both together*

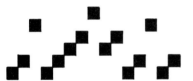

162 *Threading draft for 161*

163 *Coarse weave with doubled ends and picks*

b Distorted warp. The extra warp threads float over all the cloth, but are under the extra weft, which alternates under and over the two blocks of the warp. This is the same as (i) b but turned round weft way to warp way. It may need two warp beams.

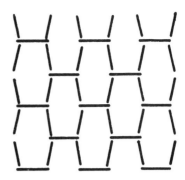

164 *Distorted warp*

165 *Threading draft for 164*

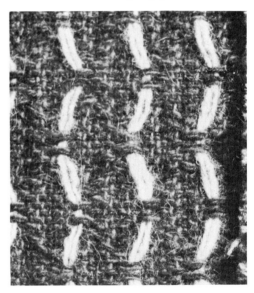

166 *Distorted warp*

(4) *Plain weave on alternate ends*

(i) Blocks of pattern on other shafts (Summer and Winter weave).

The plain warp ground is carried on the front two shafts, and the pattern blocks are carried on the rest of the shafts. When a pattern block is lifted, the alternate ends for the width of that block are raised. When one of the ground shafts is lifted it raises one out of every four ends right across the loom. By lifting together one of the ground and one of the pattern

87

shafts a $\frac{1}{3}$ weave occurs where the pattern is down, and a $\frac{3}{1}$ weave where it is up. There is, therefore, no limit to the size of the blocks. Any number of shafts may be used for the pattern, the ground is always on the front two shafts.

167   *Summer and winter weave, two block*

167a   *Summer and winter, two-block*

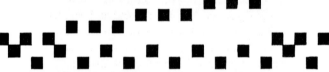

168   *Summer and winter weave, four block*

168a   *Summer and winter, four-block*

(ii)   Stitching ends on other shafts. Piqué

The ground is plain weave, and the extra warp floats mainly behind the cloth. It is brought up, in the pattern, for one pick at a time. When the first diamond has been woven, the wadding pick is inserted by lifting all the ground and sinking all the extra warp. The second diamond follows, and the wadding pick distorts between the diamonds when the fabric is washed.

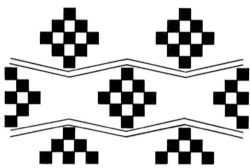

170   *Piqué*

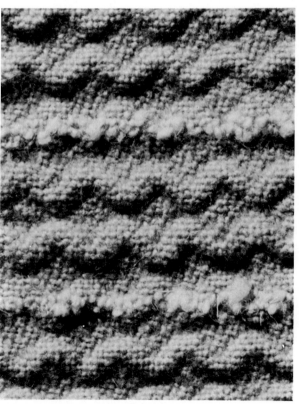

170a   *Piqué*

169 *Piqué threading draft*

(iii) Welts or ribs

The same as a Bedford cord turned from warp way to weft way. The ends on shafts 1 and 3 weave plain, while the ends on 2 and 4 float on the back and vice versa. The fabric goes into ribs across when washed. A wadding pick can be put in each rib by raising the working ends and leaving the floating ends down for it at the end of each rib.

(5) *Double plain weave*

Two cloths can be woven, one over the other, on a four shaft straight draft threading by lifting 1 and 3 alternately to weave the face cloth, and by holding 1 and 3 up and lifting 2 and 4 with them alternately to weave the back. This produces two completely separate cloths if two shuttles are used, a double width cloth if one shuttle is used and it changes between top and bottom at one edge only, and a tubular cloth if the change is at alternate edges.

(i) If alternate sections of warp are threaded on the front four and the back four shafts of an eight shaft loom, a weft may pass through the face cloth in one section and back cloth in the next, by lifting a face weave on the front set and a back weave on the back set at the same time or vice versa. By using different colours for the two different faces a two block (chess board) pattern is woven.

171 *Double plain cloth, two block, cross section*

(ii) *a* If twelve or sixteen shafts are used, three or four separately controlled sections can be woven, so that geometric patterns are possible.

The traditional Welsh double woven bed rugs are sixteen shaft weaves of this type. See colour plate facing page 48.

b To reduce the number of shafts, two harness or compound mounting is used. The figure harness at the back has the usual small-eyed heddles, and the ground harness in front has heddles with long eyes (12 cm (4½ in.)). The warp is still entered face and back alternately. The back pair of shafts of the figure harness carries the face and back ends respectively for the width of the first block, and the front pair carries the next block. The warp is then re-entered through the long-eyed ground harness, straight threading (face, back, face, back) so that each end is entered once in each harness. When the back (fourth) shaft of the figure harness is raised, it lifts all the face ends of the odd blocks, and the third lifts all the back ends of the same blocks, shafts 2 and 1 lifting face and back ends of the even blocks. The figure harness can work without being affected by the ground harness because of the long eyes of the latter. Thus when a face pick is being woven (ground shaft 4), to show on the even blocks, the back ends of the odd blocks can be raised above it, with shaft 3 of the figure harness, and the back ends of the even blocks held down below it with shaft 1. On the back pick which follows (ground shaft 3) the face ends of the even blocks are held up with shaft 2 and those of the odd blocks held down with shaft 4.

172 *Compound mounting for 171, threading draft*

89

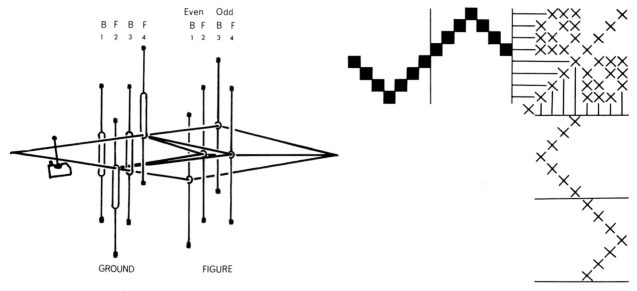

173 *Compound mounting for 171, shed showing the action of figure and ground harnesses*

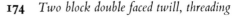

174 *Two block double faced twill, threading*

7 DOUBLE FACED WEAVES

a   Twills   Plain twill and weft way stripe.

(i) Any unbalanced twill gives a different appearance to the face and back of the cloth, one being mainly warp faced, and one mainly weft faced; a three shaft $\frac{2}{1}$ twill gives a slight difference, an eight shaft $\frac{7}{1}$ twill gives a considerable difference. Weft way stripes can be woven merely by reversing the type of twill, using a $\frac{1}{3}$ for the first stripe, and a $\frac{3}{1}$ for the second.

(ii) Two-Block

By threading the odd blocks on the back four shafts and the even blocks on the front four shafts of an eight shaft harness, warp faced $\frac{3}{1}$ and weft faced $\frac{1}{3}$ twills can alternate across and down the cloth to give checks or warp way stripes.

b   Damasks   A damask is a figured or checked fabric in a warp and weft faced weave, the figure and ground being of opposite faces, and is usually self coloured. The weave is a satin (eight or five end) or a four shaft broken twill. The damask harness (page 24) is useful for two block designs, but the two harness mounting is better for a larger number of blocks.

175 *Two block double faced twill*

90

The heddles of the figure harness have the ends for one repeat of the weave drawn together in each eye, and these ends are separated when they are entered in the ground harness (straight draft).

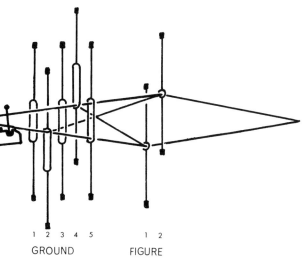

1 2 3 4 5   1 2
GROUND   FIGURE

176 *Compound mounting for two block five end damask*

177 *Threading draft for 176*

The figure harness forms the pattern without any weave. One ground shaft is raised, and with it one end of each repeat for the full width of the cloth. This gives a weft faced weave on the areas sunk, and does not affect those raised. Another ground shaft is sunk at the same time to make the warp faced weave for the raised areas, leaving the sinking areas unaffected.

c Double weft faced cloth This type of cloth has a weft faced weave on both sides, the stitching points of one being covered by the weft floats of the other. This weave can, but need not necessarily be, the same on both sides, e.g. as $\frac{1}{3}$ twill can be backed by a $\frac{3}{1}$ twill or a $\frac{2}{2}$ twill, and can be woven on four shafts.

d Double warp faced cloth Similar in construction, but with two warps and one weft. This weave needs one set of shafts for each face.

178 *Double weft faced cloth, cross section*

8   ALL OVER TEXTURED WEAVES

a Honeycomb Sunk squares formed because of the varying tensions in the threads created by the weaving. On four shafts upwards to eight, a practical limit. Point draft, and the lifting plan is always on the same principle. There are several variations, usually needing eight to sixteen shafts. Add 25 per cent to 35 per cent for take-up.

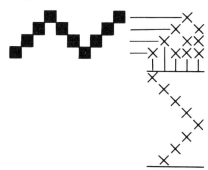

179 *Honeycomb, four shaft*

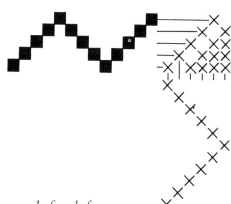

180 *Honeycomb, five shaft*

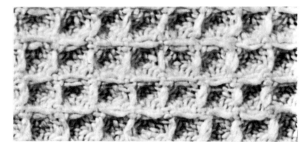

180a *Honeycomb, five-shaft*

91

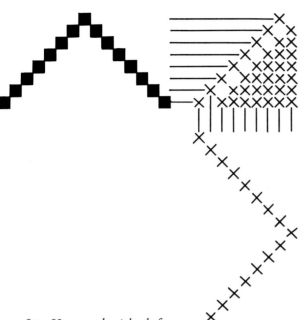

183 *Mock leno*

184 *Mock leno*

181 *Honeycomb, eight shaft*

b Mock leno or imitation gauze

   (i) Canvas weave The ends and picks run into groups of five when washed. The unit may be three, five, or seven threads, and a space may be left in the reed between the adjacent units. used commercially for embroidery canvas etc.

9 BLOCK WEAVES

a Mock leno on a ground. (*Swedish lace*) The lifting gives either or both of the pattern blocks in mock leno, with a plain border and a plain weave cross border at the ends.

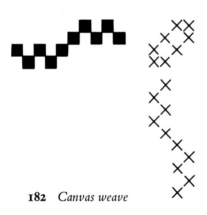

182 *Canvas weave*

   (ii) Mock leno Uses the same unit of weave, but separates the units by a single thread instead of reversing alternate units (*183, 184*).

c Huckaback Uses a similar unit to the canvas weave, but the unit alternates with plain weave and not with a reversed unit. Can be reduced or enlarged, or woven with fewer picks than ends.

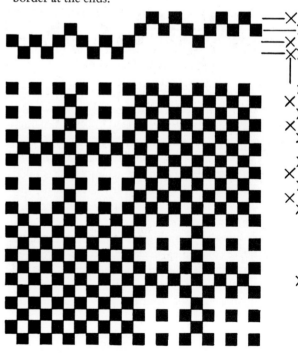

185 *Two block mock leno* (*Swedish lace*)

b Ms *and* Os two block and four shaft. Gives blocks of $\frac{4}{4}$ weave alternately with plain weave. The edges of the blocks curve slightly when washed.

Three block and five shaft. (Modified Ms and Os.)

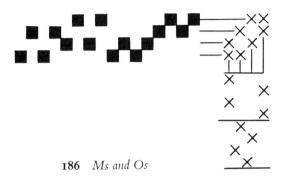

186 *Ms and Os*

186b *Ms and Os. A different lifting plan gives a totally different effect*

c Poor man's damask Useful in self colour or with a different coloured pattern weft.

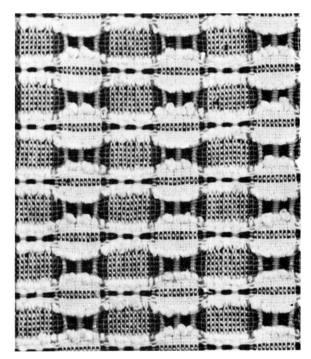

186a *Ms and Os (see also colour plate facing page 97)*

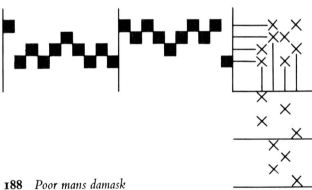

188 *Poor mans damask*

187 *Modified Ms and Os, five shaft*

93

10 COLOUR AND WEAVE EFFECTS See colour plate facing page 72.

This group of weaves is used in fabrics in which each thread is seen, as the design depends on the colour of the threads and where they are placed in relation to the weave. They can be worked out before being woven by filling in the weave plan lightly on point paper (squared paper), indicating the order of colouring above and to the left of the weave plan, and then marking the correct colour in each square, according to whether the end or pick is uppermost for that square, working down the ends first, and then across the picks.

189 *Colour and weave, showing light and dark thread marked on the upper and left edges; top left weave plan marked; top right dark ends marked; bottom left dark picks marked; bottom right final weave plan*

(i) Plain weave designs
  Basket weave This is a 1 and 1 warp and weft colouring in blocks, with a double colour to change the sequence.
  Dog tooth 2 and 2 warp and weft.

Basket weave 2 and 2 warp and weft.
Dog tooth 4 and 4 warp and weft.

(iii) *Miscellaneous*
  Gun club check, 4, 4, 4, 4, light, medium, dark, medium.
  Glen Urquhart check, a colour and weave check effect in either plain weave with stripes of 1 and 1, and 2 and 2 colouring in warp and weft, or in 2 and 2 twill, 2 and 2 and 4 and 4 colouring in warp and weft.
  Shepherd's check or plaid. The same as twill dog tooth.

11 GAUZE WEAVES

This is the class of weaves in which the one end (the crossing end) of each pair crosses from side to side of the other, (standard or standing) end, each cross being held in place by a pick of weft. Add 30 per cent to 50 per cent for take-up and up to 100 per cent on crossing warp.

The black (crossing) ends go through shaft 4 (back crossing shaft), under the white (standing ends) and then through the doup which has been threaded through the front crossing shaft. The white ends go through shaft 3 (the standard shaft), and then straight through to the cloth. Both ends of a pair must be sleyed in the same dent of the reed. The right half of the warp has the black crossing ends all going from right to left, the left half has the crossing ends alternately from the right and from the left.

There are three sheds, standard, open and crossed.

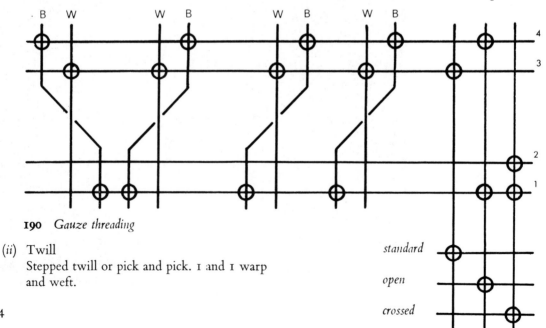

190 *Gauze threading*

(ii) Twill
  Stepped twill or pick and pick. 1 and 1 warp and weft.

standard

open

crossed

The standard and open give plain weave, standard and crossed give plain weave in the crossed position, and open and crossed give gauze weave. Leno weaves are a mixture of gauze and plain weave.

Standard shed (S) shaft 3 is raised to lift the white standing ends.

191 *Gauze, standard shed S*

Open shed (O) shaft 4 is raised to lift the black crossing ends, and shaft 1, the doup shaft, is raised at the same time to allow the doups to run through the eyes of shaft 2 and rise with the crossing ends.

192 *Gauze, open shed O*

Crossed shed (X) shafts 1 and 2 are raised together so that the doup pulls the black crossing end under the white end and up on the crossed side.

193 *Gauze, crossed shed X*

The upper fabric is gauze, and the lower leno in each photograph; the right half has the ends crossing the same way and the left has them crossing alternately right and left. The gauze is woven O, X, O, X. The leno, O, S, O, S, O, X, i.e. five plain rows and one crossed. It is immaterial which of the back two shafts is used by either end, both ways having their own advantages and disadvantages.

The fabric stretched on the loom.

The fabric slack, showing the amount of distortion that occurs.

The back of the same fabric, showing the path of the black ends.

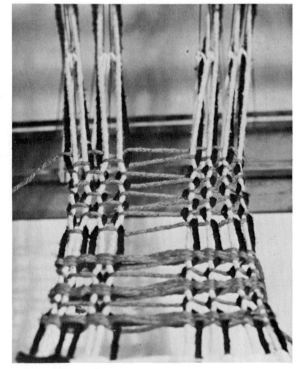

194 *Fabric on loom*

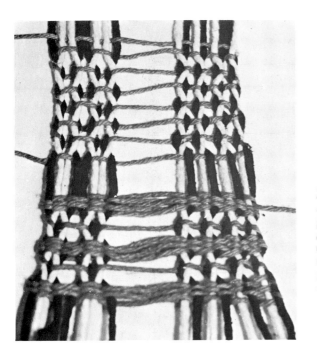

195 *Fabric off the loom*

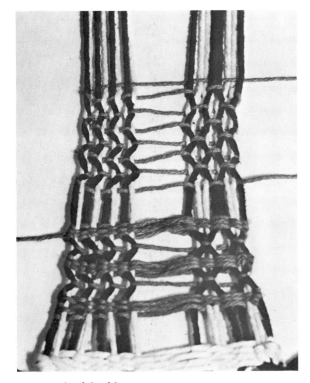

196 *Back of the fabric*

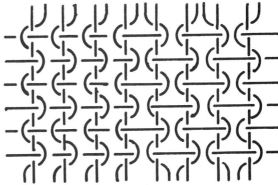

197 *Gauze cloth, weave plan*

197a *Gauze-woven cloth (open and crammed stripes)*

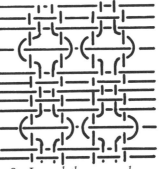

198 *Leno cloth, weave plan*

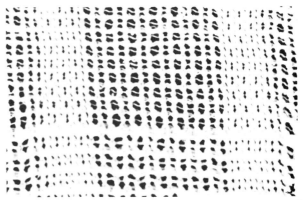

198a *Leno-woven cloth (open and crammed stripes)*

a Inlay or Brocade

(*i*) Brocading was originally a technique in which small figures were woven with separate shuttles on a plain or ornamental background. Later figures were woven with shuttles which went from side to side of the cloth, the weft between the figures floating on the back, sometimes being left, less frequently being cut away. This technique is still useful today; one variation of it is the Scandinavian dukagang.

A threading which will give $\frac{1}{3}$ or $\frac{1}{4}$ is used. After each ground row the figuring shuttles are passed down into the shed, through the width of the figure and up out of the shed, using one shuttle for each figure. The cloth is woven face downwards, so that the ends, joins etc. are on the back of the finished cloth. The width of the figures is altered by entering or leaving the shed between different sets of warp threads.

(*ii*) This is similar, but the figuring weft follows the (plain weave) ground *in the same shed*. The colours and design are not so strong as in (*i*).

(*iii*) The single figuring shuttle is passed in and out of the top part of the shed right across the loom, leaving floats between the figures. These floats are later clipped round the edges of the figure, making a heavier outline, when the yarn frays in the finishing. This is woven face upwards.

b *Free shuttle and free design* This is a modified form of inlay, in which a shuttle with a thick weft passes in and out of a $\frac{1}{3}$ shed, so that lines or solid figures are woven by the shuttle over the ground. Vertical lines are made in a similar way by passing the yarn under every fourth weft thread before it is finally beaten up.

c *Curved weft* Instead of the weft lying straight across the cloth, it follows a curved path. Flat triangular or wedge shapes are built up with the previous colours, and when the weft is laid loosely above them, it follows the shapes below it. See colour plate facing page 73.

200 *Tapestry with curved weft*

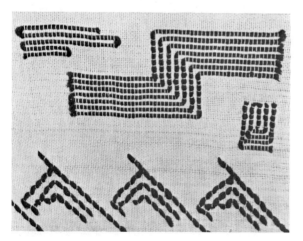

199 *Free shuttle design*

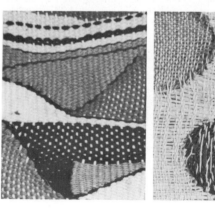

201 *Students experimental curved weft samples*

d Miscellaneous The three examples were woven on the same warp, the first shows a hand crossed gauze weave and warp threads distorted in groups by a free soumak weave. The second has cane inserted to give the twist to the groups of weft. The dark threads help to retain the warp and weft threads in their groups. The third has different materials woven in blocks on a plain weave.

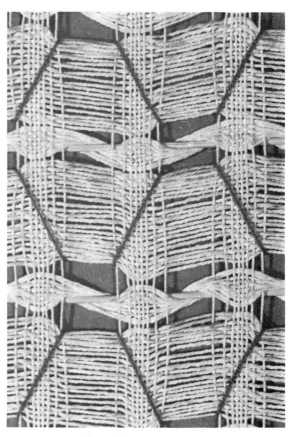

203 *Cane in the weft to produce distortion*

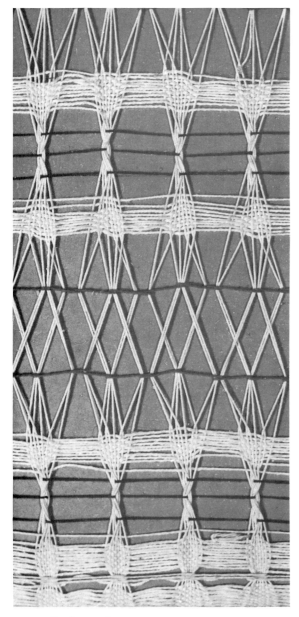

202 *Hand crossed gauze*

204 *Blocks of plain weave*

Wall hangings and decorative panels

A type of work which has become increasingly popular is that of weaving decorative panels and hangings. The more mundane requirements can be forgotten, and the imagination given more scope than is usually possible. The technique is very free, and often only slightly related to weaving. Design should always be a product of the technique of the craft as well as of the imagination, and a good designer will work within the limitations of the technique that he is employing, without trying to force the technique beyond its normal limits. In these panels the techniques are so simple, and have so few inherent limitations, that the imagination is almost entirely unrestricted; often existing techniques are modified considerably in the course of a single piece of work to find a way to express a particular idea that could not otherwise be used. Whether the work is planned in detail beforehand, or results from a freely growing design, the result should be as free as a piece of painting or sculpture, although in a totally different medium.

It is possible to use as well as weaving, a variety of other techniques, such as braids, plaits, crossed weaves, netting, pillow lace ground, in fact anything which will give the required quality of texture and pattern. The warp can be a major part of the fabric itself, or

may be little more than a framework on which to work a selection of weft materials. Double fabrics can be introduced, the lower, more solid layer providing a background for the upper layer. This technique can be extended to include woven panels which have a considerable depth, projecting from the wall five or six inches in certain areas. (A completely double panel, with a top and bottom layer held apart by the frame, is woven as two separate fabrics.)

Almost any type of material can be used. The warp, when it forms a considerable part of the design, should usually be fairly coarse; coir, coarse and fine sea grass, thick loom cord, linen rug warp, thick cotton, macrame twine, terylene twine, rayon cord, sisal, jute, raffia can be used. Rug wool is less useful, as it is too soft and indefinite for this type of work, though it can be used to fill in solid areas in the weft. Also useful in the weft are slivers or rovings of jute, hemp, terylene, fibro, rayon, etc., and carded fleece. Rushes and cane provide means of stiffening certain areas, as well as adding their own textures.

The examples which follow give some idea of the infinite variety of this freer style of weaving. They vary from the highly technical, demanding a special loom, to the technically simple, needing no more than a frame.

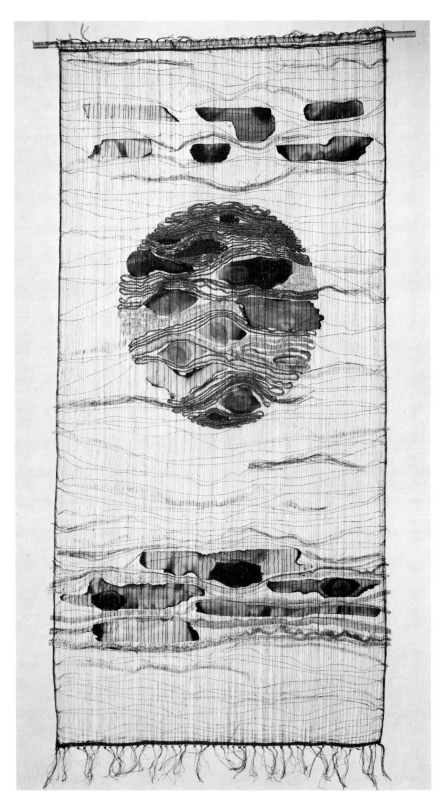

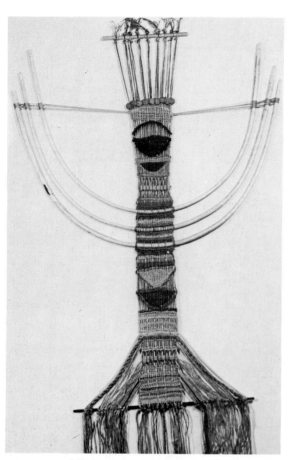

207 *Ram's Head*
by Tadek Beutlich

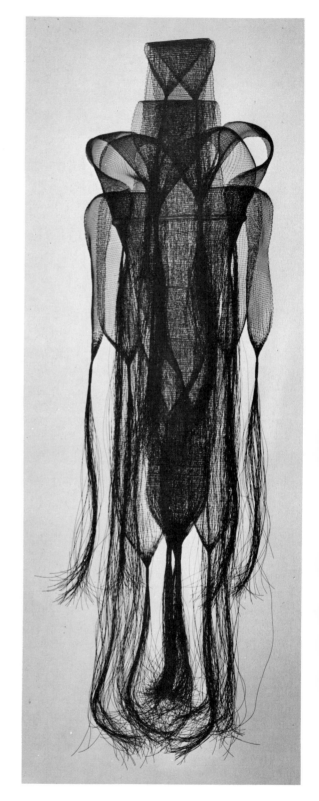

208 *Katsure*
by Kay Sekimachi

209 *Detail from Woven Waves*
by Moik Scheile

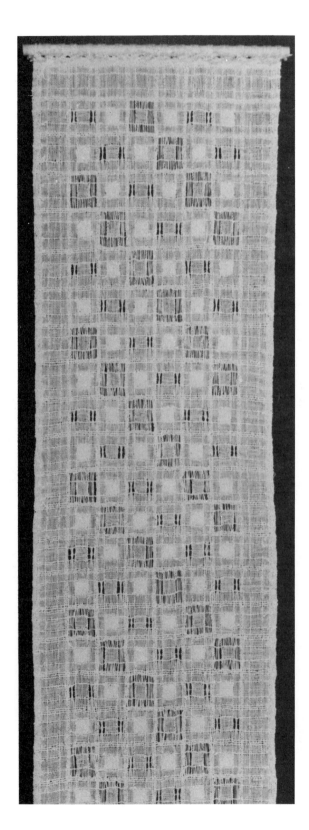

210 *and* **211** *Hangings by Vyvian Western*

Opposite
212 *Trees by Theo Moorman*

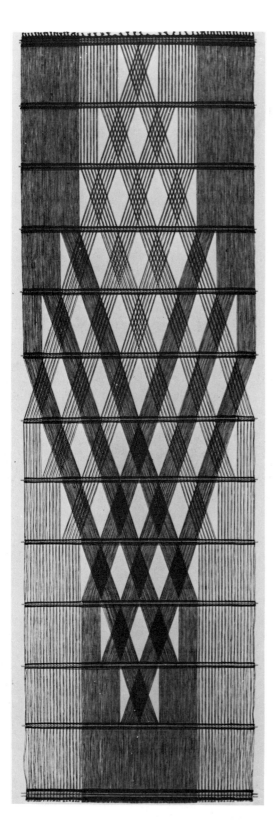

Page 106

213 *Macrogauze 29*
by Peter Collingwood

214 *Macrogauze 35*
by Peter Collingwood

Specialised techniques for the rigid heddle

1 Warping

Because of differences between the rigid heddle and shaft loom, certain processes in preparing the loom can be modified. Warping is done as usual, though only the porrey cross is needed. The warp is chained from the end without the cross, and the cross sticks put in, but not the back stick.

2 Spreading

Spreading is done through the rigid heddle itself, the loops of warp being drawn through the dents of the heddle, and then put onto the back stick. This is better than threading fully straight away and having to tie the warp on to the warp roller, as the knots spoil the tension and waste warp.

The warp is tied to a peg across the table, and the rigid heddle put into the clamp. The back stick has a length of cotton tied to it, as if for a cross stick, and is left ready for the loops to be slipped on after spreading. The warp must be placed centrally in the heddle, and this must be worked out to ascertain the starting point for threading.

A bunch of warp threads is held on the last two fingers of the left hand, and the reed hook is held in the right. The first loop of warp is picked up by the right hand from the cross sticks and drawn out of the bunch in the left hand and placed over the thumb and first two fingers. The second finger holds the thread against the thumb, and the upper part of the loop is kept taut.

The left hand is turned over, the first finger moved away from the thumb, and the thread drawn out. This thread is taken on the reed hook and brought through the upper part of the dent of the heddle.

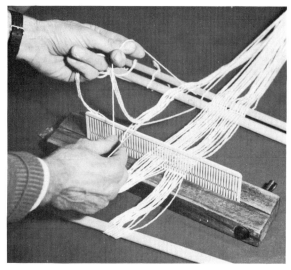

215 *Spreading the warp   1 the loop picked up*

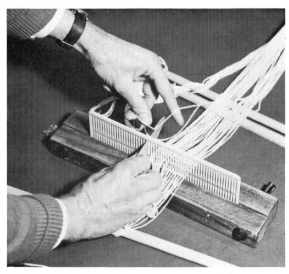

216 *Spreading the warp   2 the loop hooked*

The right hand pulls the hook downwards, the left forefinger is raised to lift the thread, while the thumb releases the thread that it was holding and is brought over the heddle to pick up the loop from the reed hook.

217 *Spreading the warp   3 the loop drawn through*

The thread is released from the hook with a slight downwards movement, and as the right hand is brought back over the heddle, the right little finger picks up the loop from the left thumb

218 *Spreading the warp   4 transferred to the little finger*
108

When the bunch on the right little finger becomes too large for comfort, it is transferred to the back stick.

As soon as all the loops have been drawn through the dents of the heddle and placed on the back stick, the free end of the string that is tied to the back stick is tied to the other end of the stick to prevent the loops slipping off. The warp is slipped off the peg and, with the heddle and block, turned completely round. The loom is placed on the table, and may have the front roller hooked over the peg, from which the warp has just been removed on the far side of the table, to prevent it slipping forward towards the weaver whilst rolling on. The two ends of the back stick are tied on to the apron, and the warp spread evenly along the stick and centrally in the loom; then the remaining ties are fastened. The reef knot is used, with one end making a half bow for ease of untying, and this loop and both ends must be pressed down between the back and apron sticks to prevent unevenness of tension.

3   Winding on

The heddle, still in its block, is placed against the roller, and the warp is held tightly 1.25 or 1.50 m (4 or 5 ft) from the loom, and stretched to even the loops round the back stick; then one full turn is taken round the roller. If the warp is the full width of the loom, the roller is locked with the wing nut, and sections of warp pulled down to tighten it. If the warp is appreciably narrower, the roller can be held by one hand, whilst the other hand stretches the sections of warp. This is continued until all but about 40 cm (15 in.) of warp is on the roller.

When the warp has been wound on, the cross is in front of the heddle. To transfer it to the back, the cross stick nearer the heddle is turned on its edge, and a spare stick placed in the same shed but *behind* the heddle. The cross stick is now withdrawn, replaced alongside the spare cross stick at the back of the heddle, and tied in immediately. The second cross stick is now turned on edge, and the process repeated. The photograph shows the first stick transferred, and the spare cross stick in position behind the heddle before the withdrawal of the second cross stick.

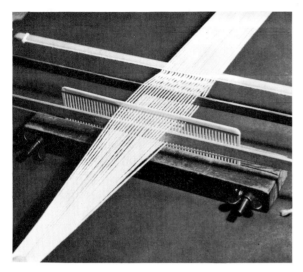

219 *Transferring the cross*

4 Threading

After the cross is transferred, the end of the warp is cut, and all the threads from below the nearer stick of the cross tied off in bunches, as they are in the correct dents. The threads from above the cross stick can also be tied off for safety.

The first bunch of warp threads is lifted to the top of the dent, and the threading hook put through the eye to the right of the dent in which is the first thread. The hook is pointed slightly to the left, underneath the first thread of the warp.

The left hand is brought down, and the end thread is caught on the hook.

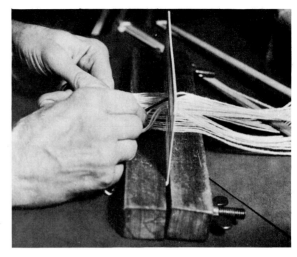

221 *Threading the eyes   2 warp lowered onto hook*

The hook is withdrawn slightly to the right, and then upwards drawing the thread through the eye.

220 *Threading the eyes   1 warp raised and hook through heddle*

222 *Threading the eyes   3 thread drawn through heddle*

This is continued until the first bunch of threads has been used, when the bunch is tied off in a loop, and the second bunch is untied ready for use. After the whole warp has been entered, the block is taken off the heddle, the loom turned the right way round, and the warp tied on. The centre bunch is taken first, about 7 cm (2½ in.) wide, then the selvedges, about 2 or 3 cm (1 in.) wide, and finally the remaining threads, divided into bunches of about 7 cm (2½ in.), are tied on. With a narrow warp it may be necessary to undo the original centre bunch after tying the selvedges and divide it between the two sides.

If the work of spreading etc. is liable to be interrupted, the warp can be tied round the front roller, the heddle supported on two strings threaded through the end dents or eyes and tied between the breast and back bars at the sides, and the loops drawn through as before. The loom may then be put away at any time without fear of spoiling the warp. The winding on can be done through the heddle, and transferring the cross, and the final threading and tying on all done without untying the heddle.

5 Weaving

Weaving is done by alternately raising and depressing the heddle. Raising it presents no problem, but often the fingers of the hand used to press it down rest below the top of the heddle, and slightly lower the warp threads, which then catch on the prongs of the shuttle, or can go under the shuttle instead of over it.

Care must be taken with the selvedges. Sufficient weft for the row about to be woven must be undone from the shuttle. If this is not done, the sudden check in the shed will pull the selvedge in sharply, and tighten up the weft for at least 3 cm (1 in.) in the previous row. This is bound to happen occasionally, and when it does the row being woven should be taken out, the shed reversed and the previous row retensioned. Certain of the weaves in the next sections have floats at the selvedges, causing intermittent missing of some of the selvedge threads. When this occurs, the shuttle should be placed the wrong side of the end thread, whether up or down, and brought into the shed from there; i.e. if the first thread is in the top shed, the shuttle goes above it, and down into the shed, and vice versa.

The neatest way of fastening off the beginning of a yarn is to leave an end of about 20 mm (¾ in.) at the beginning of the first row, and turn this into the second shed with the second row of weft, after it has been beaten into place. The only way of ending a yarn is to go the wrong side of the outside selvedge thread as explained above, and put 20 mm (¾ in.) of thread in the same shed as the last row. The end should never be put in the following shed, as is done with the beginning, as it will be alongside a different colour and will show up badly. When joining the same colour, all that is needed is to overlap 20 mm (¾ in.) of old and new yarn, and if they have been broken and not cut, the tapering of the end helps to make the join less noticeable. This join can be made at the selvedge, if less obtrusive there, by turning the old yarn into the new shed and leaving an end of the new yarn hanging out, this end being trimmed off flush with the selvedge after the next few rows have been woven.

The rigid heddle is fundamentally a plain weave loom, but much may be done to give variety to the work produced on it. Plain warps may be spaced or grouped, and thick and thin threads used. Threads can be doubled or trebled to give cord or rib effects, and a double thread used to weave hopsack. The basket weave, dogtooth, and glen check colour and weave effects are straightforward, and the one and one stepped twill or pick and pick can be woven in a hopsack weave by having a light and dark thread in each pair of threads which work together in both warp and weft.

There is a whole range of weaves usually woven on four, or sometimes more shafts, which can be produced on the rigid heddle by using a stick or sticks threaded into the warp to give the extra sheds necessary. Some are no slower than plain weave, and none are too slow to be of practical use.

a Extra weft This is a second weft yarn, usually somewhat thicker and softer than the main weft, running more over the surface of the fabric than through it, and which could be cut out without destroying the fabric on which it is used. It is usually caught down or stitched about every 5 mm (¼ in.), which on a rigid heddle means every fourth thread. These stitching threads are raised by a stick which is kept in the warp behind the heddle at the back of the loom. To insert the stick the heddle is pulled down from underneath, bringing the threads in the dents uppermost. The alternate threads of this set are now picked up on a warp stick behind the heddle. When this stick is brought forward to the heddle and turned on edge, the threads over it are raised and the rest depressed, bringing one thread up and leaving the next three down. When the stick is returned to the back of the loom it does not interfere with the normal shedding. This produces an all-over weave across the width of the fabric.

The same weave can be used to produce a two block (check) pattern. A main pattern stick is put into the warp as for the all-over weave, to ensure that the same threads are used for stitching throughout the weave. A second stick is put through the normal down shed for the width of the first block, and then through the stick shed for the width of the second block. This sequence is repeated as often as required across the cloth. Only the second stick is used for weaving. Two weft threads are used, the pattern weft again being somewhat thicker and softer than the ground. Two rows of ground are followed by a single pattern row using the second stick on its edge.

The second check is woven in the same way, but with the pattern stick threaded in the opposite way, i.e. through the pattern stick shed of the first block, and the normal down shed for the second block. The stick used for the first block, and of course the main pattern stick, need not be removed from the warp, though the second pattern stick has to be taken out at the end of the block and re-inserted when needed.

Patterns consisting of a figure on a plain ground can be woven by putting the pattern stick through the normal shed for the ground, and picking up only what is required for the figure in the centre.

b Distorted weft This is a simple pattern to weave, as most of it is plain cloth. The main pattern stick is picked up as before, taking the alternate threads of those in the dents. A first pattern stick picks up the alternate threads of those already over the main stick. This stick is now kept touching the back of the heddle while weaving 15 mm ($\frac{1}{2}$ in.) of plain cloth, so that the threads over it are not woven in at all for that distance, the stick being lifted by the threads in the eyes of the heddle on the up shed. The main stick is now brought forward on its edge to the back of the heddle, coming under the first pattern stick, and a row of thick, soft yarn put loosely through the shed. The main and first pattern sticks are now pushed to the back of the

loom, and a second pattern stick picks up the threads which were over the main stick but under the first pattern stick. This stick is now kept flat at the back of the heddle for a further 15 mm ($\frac{1}{2}$ in.), when it is withdrawn and the main stick used on its edge for the thick weft again. This sequence is repeated continuously, i.e. the first pattern stick touching the heddle for 15 mm ($\frac{1}{2}$ in.), the main stick on edge for the thick weft, second pattern stick for 15 mm ($\frac{1}{2}$ in.), main stick on edge etc.

223 *Distorted weft effects woven on a rigid heddle loom*

III

When the tension is taken off, the long floats of warp distort the thick weft thread up and down, giving a cellular effect on the surface of the cloth. The weave may be varied by picking up two and missing one on the first pattern stick, and the opposite on the second stick, or by using the pattern sticks to make the warp floats but omitting every other thick weft. This gives a series of zig-zag weft threads, running across the cloth.

c *Mock leno* This weave needs only one stick at the back of the heddle. With the heddle down, pick up two and miss one right across. If the stick is kept touching the heddle, the down shed is unaffected, but on the up shed the stick is held up by the threads in the eyes. As long as the stick is kept against the heddle, the threads over it are not woven in. The weaving must start with a down row, and continue for a total of five rows, with the stick touching the heddle. On the sixth row, an up row, the stick is moved back, and the threads over it are allowed to weave in. The first five rows should be fairly closely beaten, and the sixth lightly beaten. The weave does not show until the fabric is washed, as it depends on the grouping or running together of the threads, caused by the warp and weft floats. The size of unit can be varied by picking up one or three instead of two, and still missing one only, and by having three or seven rows before the last up row without the stick.

To weave two block check pattern, pick up two and miss one for the first and subsequent odd numbered blocks, and carry the stick over all the even numbered blocks, and weave as before. This gives alternate stripes of mock-leno and plain weave. When the first block is long enough, push the stick to the back of the loom, and with a second stick pick up the even blocks and omit the odd blocks. A main stick picked up right across is again helpful to ensure that groups of threads are kept the same throughout the weave, and there are no half groups left at the edges of the blocks. Patterns with any number of small squares can be woven by keeping the stick on top of the warp for the ground, and picking up only where required for the mock-leno weave.

An alternative way of weaving mock-leno is to pick up one and miss two of the threads in the dents and then weave, heddle up and stick on edge for five rows and then finishing with a down row. This brings the other face of the cloth onto the top. To weave a two block pattern by this method, the stick is put through the down shed for the width of the plain blocks.

d *Huckaback* This weave consists of one unit of mock-leno, and a block of plain weave of the same number of threads, alternating warp way and weft way, and the method of weaving it is very similar to that of mock-leno. With the heddle down, pick up two, miss four right across the loom. Then turn the loom over, pull the heddle downwards in its new position, and with a stick pick up two and miss four again, the two taken the second time being the centre threads of the four missed from the first stick. Five threads are now woven with each stick; with only the top stick against the heddle, start with a down shed and weave five rows, then reverse the sticks, and with the bottom stick against the heddle, start with an up shed and weave five more rows. The weave must always start with a shed away from the stick, i.e. if the top stick is against the heddle, the first shed is down, and vice versa.

e *Canvas weave* The canvas weave has the same five thread unit as huckaback, but instead of alternating with plain weave, a weft faced unit and a warp faced unit alternate. The two sticks are put in as for huckaback, and with *both* sticks against the heddle four rows are woven, starting with a down shed. Then the sticks are pushed back, and two more rows woven, maintaining the sequence of down and up. This is not exactly the normal canvas weave, but is sufficiently like it in general effect.

f *Gauze and leno* See illustrations 195 to 198. A gauze or crossed weave is one in which one warp end of each pair takes half a turn round the second one of the pair, between each row of weft. This half cross holds the weft in place, so both setting in the heddle and beating can be spaced out without detriment to the cloth. The simplest form of gauze is woven with alternate pairs of warp threads omitted from the heddle, and the right-hand thread of each pair in an eye. The last row of plain weave before the gauze should be an up row. A smooth warp stick, preferably pointed at the end, is needed to pick up the threads on the crossed row; the open row which alternates with it is always an up shed.

Rest the point of the stick on the first of the threads in the dents on the right of the heddle, and with the left hand take the other thread of the pair (in the eye) and draw it across to the left below the thread in the dent on which the stick is resting, and then up to the left of that thread, and put it on the stick. Slide the stick one thread further on, and again bring the eye thread which is on the right, under and up to the left of the other thread of the pair, and place it on the stick. This is repeated across the warp. Turn the stick on edge and put the shuttle through the shed so formed; push the thread lightly into place with the stick before gently beating up with the heddle. The next row is an up row, the ordinary plain weave shed.

Gauze can be combined with the plain weave to produce a fabric of open and closely woven squares. In this case the half spacing in the heddle would alternate with the normal spacing, and the gauze weave would be put in only on the openly spaced warp. An up row must precede and follow each complete section of gauze weave to hold the twist.

If every third thread of the normal threading is omitted, so that the threading goes eye, dent, dent, eye, the right-hand pair can be crossed as usual, but the eye thread of the left-hand pair is taken under and up to the right. This brings both eye threads up between the two dent threads to be placed on the stick, so that the crossing is alternately left hand and right hand. The second row is still a plain up shed. This fabric is more elastic than the plain gauze, and has a more decorative effect. If each crossed row is followed by five plain rows, beginning and ending with an up row, this is a true leno weave, of which mock-leno is an imitation. This particular six thread leno weave is well known both as a cellular blanket weave and a summer weight cotton fabric.

Glossary

Apron The cloth on the rollers of the loom to which the warp is secured.

Apron sticks Sticks in the hem of the apron to strengthen it.

Batten The swinging frame which carries the reed and shuttle race.

Batten, overslung Pivoted on the top rail or cape of the loom.

Batten, underslung Pivoted below the warp.

Batten-cap The loose, grooved bar of wood which holds the top of the reed.

Beam A roller or a bar across the loom.

Beam, back The beam over which the warp runs from the roller to the shafts.

Beam, breast The beam over which the cloth runs at the front of the loom.

Beam, cloth The front roller which holds the finished cloth.

Beam, warp The back roller which holds the warp.

Beaming Winding the warp onto the warp beam.

Binder 1 An extra warp used to tie down long weft floats in figured weaving.
    2 An American term for the ground weft in pattern weaving.

Block A unit of pattern, particularly in pattern weaves based on squares.

Bobbin A flanged tube to carry the weft.

Border A strip running lengthways down the edges of the cloth and needing a different threading from the rest of the cloth.

Border, cross A strip running across the cloth and needing a different lifting or treadling from the rest of the cloth.

Bout A group of threads warped together.

Bowcord The cord tied along the top heddle stick and by which it is suspended from any central lifting mechanism.

Brocade Cloth with figures woven in with separate shuttles (see inlay).

Burling Taking out burrs (vegetable impurities), and bringing knots to the back of the cloth before finishing.

Cape The top rail of the side of the loom.

Castle Short serrated wooden bars to hold the shafts while threading.

Castle, top See top-castle.

Chain The warp after it has been removed from the mill and chained up.

Cheese A round package of yarn.

Cone A conical package of yarn.

Cop A cylindrical package of yarn with a conical end, and unsupported except for the lowest 8 cm (3 in.).

Count The size of the yarn expressed as a ratio between the length and weight.

Counter balanced A mounting in which the rising motion results from the sinking motion, and is not positively operated.

Counter march See march.

Couper The levers on the top-castle to give the rising motion to the shafts.

Crabbing A finishing process for worsted. (See page 117).

Creel The rack for holding yarn packages for warping.

Cropping Cutting the raised surface to correct even length.

Cross Interlacing of warp threads either singly or in groups to keep them in order.

Cross, Porrey The cross in single threads used for threading the heddles.

Cross, Portée The cross in groups for raddling or beaming.

Cross sticks Sticks placed through the cross to retain it.

Cross border See border, cross.

Cut 300 yards skein used in Galashiels count. (See page 77).

Damask A cloth in which the warp and weft faced satins alternate, giving (1) a weft faced figure on a warp faced ground, and (2) squares or rectangles of warp and weft faced satin.

Denier The standard weight for counting continuous filament yarns.

Dent The space between two wires in the reed.

Dobby A device for selecting and lifting the shafts in a predetermined order, and using only one treadle.

Dolly A small skein of yarn, wound figure-of-eight on the thumb and finger, used in rug and coarse tapestry weaving and in inlay.

Doubling Plying.

Doup 1 The half heddle used in gauze weaving.
    2 The long loops above and below the eye of a string heddle.

Draft 1 Diagrammatic representation of threading or treadling.
    2 The order of threading itself.

Drawing-in See entering.

Dressing the loom All the processes preparatory to weaving.

Drop box Two or more shuttle boxes on a fly shuttle batten to enable several shuttles to be used at will.

End A warp thread.

Entering The process of drawing the warp ends through the eyes of the heddles.

Eye Any small hole or loop through which a thread passes especially the small loop in the centre of the heddle.

Fell   The edge of the cloth where the last pick has been beaten-up.

Filling   The American term for weft.

Finishing   The process such as scouring, milling, raising, cropping, etc. that a cloth undergoes after burling and mending.

Float   A short length of thread passing over two or more threads of the other set.

Flush   See float.

Fly shuttle   A shuttle propelled across the loom by pulling a cord, so that wider cloths can be woven (See pages 25, 28 and 29).

Fold   See ply.

Fulling   Obsolete term for milling (q.v.).

Gating   Adjusting the mounting of a loom.

Hank   A measure of length (840 yards) used in the cotton count.

Harness   A complete set of shafts of heddles. Also an American term for shaft.

Harness, compound   A harness in two or more parts, each of which has a separate function, such as making the ground or the figure.

Harness, figure   The harness which raises the figure in the large, without any weave.

Harness, ground   The harness which makes the ground sheds across the whole width of the cloth irrespective of the figures.

Heading   The waste strip of about 5 cm (2 in.) at the beginning of a piece of cloth.

Heald   See heddle.

Heck   The pair of small shafts on a warping mill for taking the porrey cross.

Heck block   The heavy block on a warping mill to which the heck and the guide rollers are fastened.

Heddle   The string or wire loop through which the warp ends are threaded, and by which they are raised or lowered.

Heddle-block   A block of wood with four pins on which the string heddles are knotted.

Heddle-stick   The sticks running through the top and bottom doups of string heddles.

Heddle-horse   The bar of wood in the upper mounting of a counter-balanced harness to which the upper heddle sticks are tied.

Horse   See heddle-horse.

Inlay   A weave in which each figure is woven in with a separate shuttle, on a plain weave ground. The inlay weave may be plain or may float and be tied down at regular intervals.

Jack   1   See Couper.
2   An old English term for horse.

Lacing   The cords attaching the back sticks to the warp and cloth beams.

Lam   An old English term for shaft.

Lamm   See march.

Lath, warp   See warp lath.

Lea   The standard length (300 yards) used in wet spun linen count.

Lease   Cross.

Leash   1   A loop or cord for lifting the far set of threads when using a shed stick *q.v.*
2   A heddle.

Mail   The metal eye in knitted string heddles.

March   1   The lever in the lower mounting which gives the rising shed on a counter-march mounting.
2   The lever in the lower mounting of a counter-balanced mounting.

March, counter   The lever which, working in opposition to the march, gives the sinking shed in a counter-march mounting.

March, long   See march 1.

March, short   See counter march.

Mending   Darning in any ends and picks which have been missed or broken in the weaving.

Milling   Working a woollen cloth in hot soap solution to mat the fibres together slightly by pressure.

Mounting   The whole of the mechanism for dividing the warp threads, including the heddles, all the cording, the coupers, pulleys, marches, etc.

Paddle   A slip of wood with two rows of holes, used for keeping the threads in order and taking the porrey cross while warping.

Pawl   The pointed tongue which engages with the toothed ratchet wheel to prevent a beam from turning.

Pedal   See treadle.

Pick   One row of weft.

Piece   A length of cloth, formerly 60 yards.

Pile   The threads standing up at right angles to the surface of the cloth in velvet or rugs.

Pile, uncut   Loops as above.

Pirn   1   Small cylindrical yarn package unwinding over the end, for a shuttle.
2   The tube for 1.

Ply   To twist two or more threads together.

Porrey   The sections of warp between the heddles and the cross sticks.

Portée   A group of threads warped together.

Quill   The small tube, originally a quill or reed and now made of paper, on which the bobbin for a hand shuttle is wound.

Race, shuttle   See shuttle race.

Raddle   A frame with a removable top or cap having wires or pegs set at equal intervals, used for spreading the warp to its correct width for beaming.

Raising   Brushing up the fibres on the surface of a cloth to give a nap surface.

Ratchet wheel   A toothed wheel.   See pawl.

Reed   The piece of equipment for spacing the warp and beating up the weft, and made of reed until the mid-eighteenth century.

Reed hook   A thin flat hook for threading the reed.

Retaining cord   The cord tied along a heddle-stick to prevent the heddles slipping off the end.

Rice   A skein holder standing on the floor, and having two cylindrical cages to hold the skeins.

Rocker   See couper.

Roller   See beam.

Satin   Warp faced weave without any definite diagonal line.

Satin, reverse   Weft faced weave.

Scouring   Removing the grease from woollen goods.

Selvedge   The firm edge of the cloth.

Sett   The number of warp ends to 10 cm or 4 in.

Setting up   The threading, sleying and making ready for weaving.

Shaft   One set of heddles on the sticks.

Shaft, spring   See spring shaft.

Sheave   The wheel of a pulley block.

Shed   The space between two layers of warp for the shuttle.

Shed stick   The broad stick for making the shed on a simple frame loom.

Shot   One row of weft.

Shuttle   The tool for carrying the weft.

Shuttle, fly   A heavy steel pointed shuttle driven across the loom by a leather pick in response to a pull on the cord.

Shuttle, hand   A smaller hand thrown shuttle.

Shuttle, roller   A hand shuttle with two small wooden rollers on the base.

Shuttle box   The box at the end of a fly shuttle batten for throwing and catching the shuttle.

Shuttle race   The beading on the upper surface of the race block of the batten for the shuttle to run on.

Singles   A single strand unplied yarn.

Skein   A measure of length (256 yards), used in Yorkshire woollen count.

Slabstock   The old English term for the breast beam, but also used for the back beam.

Sley   1   The part of the batten which carries the reed.
　　　　2   Old term for reed.

Sley knives   Thick reed hooks of bone or box wood, used in pairs (see page 47).

Slider frame   The frame for wire heddles.

Spool   1   Flanged tube of yarn.
　　　　2   A small cylindrical package of yarn.

Spool rack   A frame with rods across it for holding spools for warping or winding weft bobbins.

Spring shaft   A small stabilising shaft about a quarter of the length of the heddle stick, mounted below a shaft, be-

tween it and the march on a counter balanced mounting.

Sticks, back and front   The sticks tied to the aprons or lacing, and to which the warp is tied.

Swift   Skein holder.

Sword   The swinging side supports carrying the batten.

Tabby   Plain weave.

Take-up   The amount that a warp shortens in length due to the bending of threads in weaving.

Tapestry   1   A weave in which the openly spaced warp is entirely coverd by the weft.
　　　　　2   A mural decoration in tapestry weave.

Temple or *Tenterhook*   A tool for stretching the cloth out to its full width on the loom while weaving.

Threading   See entering.

Threading hook   A long fine hook for entering.

Tie-up   1   The arrangement of cords from treadles to marches, which varies with different weaves.
　　　　2   A plan of this arrangement.

Top castle   The bearers, resting on the capes or top side members of the loom, for carrying the whole of the mounting.

Treadle   The long levers from the back to front of the loom, worked by the feet.

Twist   The spin in a yarn.   S twist, Z twist, L hand and R hand twist respectively, the direction of the fibres being the same as the centre bar of the letter designating it.

Warp   The strong threads running through the loom, and the length of the cloth.

Warp faced   A cloth in which the warp yarn predominates on the face.

Warp laths   The light sticks wound between layers of the warp while beaming.

Warping   The process of making a warp of the right length and number of threads.

Warping board   A board or frame set with pegs round which the warp is wound.

Warping mill   A cylindrical frame round which the warp is wound spirally.

Weave   The order of interlacing the ends and picks.

Web   The old term for the cloth on the loom.

Weft   The transverse threads in the cloth.

Weft faced   A cloth in which the weft threads predo-dominate on the face.

Winding on   See beaming.

Witch   Similar in principle to a dobby (*q.v.*) but differing in details.

Woof   The old term for weft.

Yarn count   See count.

Bibliography

Fabric Structure

Elementary Textile Design and Fabric Structure: John Read, Edward Arnold

Foundations of Fabric Structure: J. H. Strong, National Trade Press Limited

Textile Design and Colour: W. Watson, Longmans

Advanced Textile Design: W. Watson, Longmans

Designing on the Loom: M. Kirby, Studio

Watson's Textile Design and Colour: revised Z. Grosicki, Newnes-Butterworth

Watson's Advanced Textile Design: revised Z. Grosicki, Newnes-Butterworth

Hand Weaving Technique

Treatise on the Art of Weaving: John Murphy, Blackie

Hand Loom Weaving: L. Hooper, Pitman

The New Draw Loom: L. Hooper, Pitman

Your Hand Weaving: E. Davenport, Sylvan Press

Designers Draw Loom: A. Hindson, Faber

Manual of Swedish Hand Weaving: Ulla Cyrus, Branford

Domestic Manufacturers Assistant in the Arts of Weaving & Dyeing: J. & R. Bronson, Branford

Peter Collingwood—His Weaves & Weaving: Shuttlecraft of America, Monograph, 8

Hand Weaving and Patterns

Shuttlecraft Book of American Hand Weaving: M. M. Atwater, Macmillan

Foot Power Loom Weaving: E. F. Worst, Bruce Publishing Company

How to Weave Linens: E. F. Worst, Bruce Publishing Company

The Weavers Craft: Simpson and Weir, The Dryad Press

The Weaver's Book, Harriet Tidball, Macmillan

Pattern Books

A Handweavers Pattern Book: M. Davidson, J. Spencer Inc.

Key to Weaving: M. Black, J. Spencer Inc.

Swedish Weaving: edited by Thelma M. Nye, Batsford, Van Nostrand Reinhold

Weaves and Pattern Drafting: John Tovey, Batsford, Watson-Guptill

Weaving Patterns: M. Selander, Wezäta Forlag Goteburg

Swedish Handweaving: M. Selander, Studio

Hand Weaving Patterns from Finland: Pyysalo and Merisalo, Branford

General Books and Allied Books

Anni Albers; on Design, Weslyan University Press

Byways in Handweaving: M. Atwater, Macmillan

Your Yarn Dyeing: E. Davenport, Sylvan Press

Textiles of Ancient Peru and their Techniques: Raoul D'Harcourt, University of Washington Press

The Technique of Rug Weaving: Peter Collingwood, Faber

Anni Albers on Weaving: Weslyan University Press, Middletown, Connecticut

Rug Weaving: Klares and Hutton, Batsford

Tappisserie de Jean Lurçat: Copyright of Pierre Vormes at Belvès

Ashleys Book of Knots: C. Ashley, Faber

Quarterly Journal of the Guild of Weavers, Spinners and Dyers

C.I.B.A. Review (libraries only)

History

Historic Textile Fabrics: R. Glazier, Batsford

The Romance of Textiles: E. Lewis, Macmillan

Ancient Decorative Textiles: V. Thurston, Favil Press

Spinning and Weaving: S. E. Ellacott, Methuen

Man is a Weaver: E. C. Baity, Harrap

The Romance of French Weaving: Paul Rodier, Tudor Publishing Company

Raw Materials

An Introduction to the Study of Spinning: W. E. Morton, Longmans

British Pure-bred Sheep: National Sheep Breeders Association

Sheep: J. F. H. Thomas, Faber

International Wool Secretariat Publications, Dorland House, 18–20 Regent Street, S.W.1

Cotton Board, The Royal Exchange, Manchester 2

British Man-made Fibres Federation, 58 Whitworth Street, Manchester

Your Hand Spinning: E. Davenport, Sylvan Press

Fabrics for Needlework: R. P. Giles, Methuen

Pitmans Common Industries and Commodities Series
   Silk: L. Hooper
   Linen: Moore
   Wool: Hunter
   Worsted: Dumville and Kershaw

Index

Illustration numbers are in *italics*